THE ADVISORY BOARD PLAYBOOK

NANCY MAYER

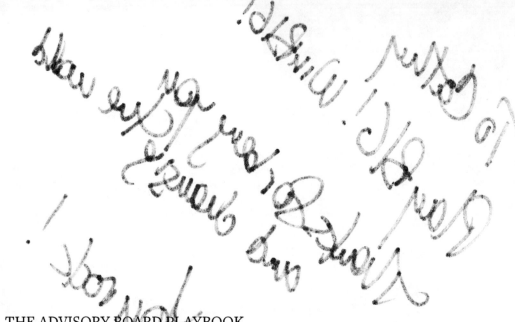

THE ADVISORY BOARD PLAYBOOK

© 2022 Nancy Mayer

All rights reserved. No part of this publication may be reproduced, distributed, or transmitted in any form or by any means, including photocopying, recording, or other electronic or mechanical methods, without the prior written permission of the publisher, except in the case of brief quotations embodied in critical reviews and certain other noncommercial uses permitted by copyright law. For permission requests, write to the publisher, addressed "Attention: Permissions Coordinator" at the address below:

Nancy Mayer
Huntsville, UT
nancymbusiness@gmail.com

Ordering Information:

Special discounts are available on quantity purchases by corporations, associations, educational institutions, and others. For details, contact Nancy Mayer above.

Printed in the United States of America

Cover and interior design: Maria Biaggini

Cover image: Rawpixel, Depositphoto

First Edition

ISBN 978-1-5136-9343-9

Publisher: Winsome Entertainment Group LLC

"As an investor and the founder of VentureCapital.com since the 70s, I have seen the magic that happens when a variety of mentors / advisors collaborate to help founders solve a specific challenge. In this book, Nancy has been able to formalize a step-by-step process to get the right advisors at the table and apply their collective knowledge to create innovative solutions."

~ **Brad Bertoch,**
Founder of VentureCapital.org

"Nancy is a true professional with a passion for helping businesses and organizations thrive in pursuit of their mission. This shines through in *The Advisory Board Playbook* where she clearly outlines the purpose and need for an advisory board. As the chairman of Angel Investors Network, an active investor myself, and serial entrepreneur, I know firsthand how important having the right advisors on your team can be! Forming a company is no easy feat, and no one should attempt to go it alone. With so many people who have come before us and weathered the battlefield of business, why wouldn't we want to seek their advice and wisdom in forming or growing our venture?

Unfortunately, most founders and business owners have little experience in forming and managing an advisory board and fail to utilize one of the most influential and powerful tools they could find! An advisory board acts based on Napoleon Hill's *mastermind* principle, and any founder, owner, or executive director would be wise to pick up and read *The Advisory Board Playbook* to harness this incredible power to achieve success in your organization!"

~ **Jeff Barnes,**
President of the Angel Investor Network and best-selling author of
The Ultimate Guide to Self-Directed Investing & Retirement Planning, and *All Hands on Deck*

"As the founder of The NGO Whisperer™ and a Global Consultant working with not-for-profits worldwide, I highly recommend *The Advisory Board Playbook* as a guide to anyone seeking to set up a not-for-profit advisory board for their organization. This book helps not-for-profit leaders understand both the *Why* and the *How* of leveraging great advisors to ensure that the purpose or the organization and the good work it brings to the world are optimized and that everyone involved feels valued and appreciated."

~ **Carolyne A. Opinde Dr.h.c. MSc.PMP®,**
Founder and CEO, The NGO Whisperer™

"This is a great book that should be on your shelf."

~ **Bradley Roulston,**
Fellow to the FPSC and community organizer

TABLE OF CONTENTS

Foreword by Sam Wong vii
Author's Note xiii
Introduction. 1

PART 1: THE CASE FOR ADVISORY BOARDS

Section 1 — POWER

The Power of the Advisory Board. 11

    What is an Advisory Board? 14
    The Power of Collective Thinking. 17
    The Power of Association 19
    The Power of Focus 21
    The Power of Results 23
    The Power of Action 25

Section 2 — VALUE

The Value of an Advisor 29

    What Makes a Good Advisor? 31
    The Value of Knowledge 33
    The Value of Connection 35
    The Value of Commitment 37
    The Value of Contribution. 39
    The Value of Collaboration 41

PART 2: ADVISORY BOARD BUILDER (ABB): A Proprietary 5-P Process

Overview 47

    Advisory Board Builder (ABB). 49
    Purpose. 52

Players 59
　　　Preparation 73
　　　Planning 77
　　　Performance 83

PART 3: THE ULTIMATE MEETING BLUEPRINT

The Art of the Meeting 89

　　　Preparation 96
　　　Facilitation 104
　　　Visual Communication 115
　　　Ideation and Innovation 127
　　　Gamification 132

PART 4: FOUR TYPES OF ADVISORY BOARDS

Overview 145

　　　Strategic Advisory Board — Business Solutions 148
　　　Customer Advisory Board (CAB) — Marketing Research 157
　　　Community Advisory Board — Volunteer and Fundraising Solutions . 166
　　　Peer Advisory Board — Formal Mastermind 174

Conclusion 181
About the Advisors 187
About the Author 200
The Power of Asking 202
About the Team 203

FOREWORD
By Sam Wong

I leaned in with keen curiosity when Nancy Mayer first engaged me to describe her book on advisory boards. My role as a CEO, coach, and advisor for several startups gives me a front-row seat to observe and interact with the founders and advisory boards of many companies. Nancy finished sharing the book's overview and my curiosity had its answer — this book would fill an important need for both startups and established companies.

We shared our real-world experiences and agreed upon what they had revealed — a wealth of untapped and unrealized potential could be accessed and transformed for small and large companies using advisory boards. We both believe that smart leaders integrate advisory services as a key aspect of their business operations. Every business operation or function consists of *people*, *processes*, and *tools*. In order to improve any business function, executives need to address one, two, or all three of these components. To avoid this remaining an intellectual exercise, leaders also need to build *plans* to implement the right system that produces tangible results.

People

Advisory systems consist of two parties: the advisor and the advisee. Any attempts to strengthen the people element of the system must address each party individually, along with the interplay and fit between them.

I've personally seen companies choose an advisor who doesn't have the relevant skill set. Maybe the advisor has large company experience, but the company needs small company expertise. The problems faced by a seasoned executive at a large company are very different than those in a small company. Maybe the company needs implementation help, but the advisor's strength is in strategic planning and not in front-line tactics. In some cases, I've even seen some advisors who are brilliant at their work, but aren't great teachers of their craft. Not every successful athlete has the skill set to be a great coach.

In other situations, the gaps are more with the advisee. Maybe the advisee is unable to identify their own needs and therefore unable to articulate the true nature of the pain to the advisor. Maybe the advisee is able to absorb high-level concepts, but struggles with actual implementation and follow through. In some cases, advisees feel the need to defend their every decision and action, rendering them uncoachable.

Whenever there is a situation where the people part of the system is lacking, it's usually some blend of issues on behalf of both parties involved. It may be difficult for an advisee to express their actual needs, but seasoned advisors should know how to listen and ask open-ended, probing questions to reveal the root cause issues. Or it may just be a clash of cultures or styles that result in a sub-optimal relationship.

Nancy's commitment to people and their successes drives this part of the book. She has explained the value of knowledge, connection, and collaboration, broadening limiting perspectives on what motivates people. Her clarity addresses many of the people issues that otherwise interfere with good work.

Processes

In the startup space, very few advisors use a roadmap or framework to guide their coaching and teaching. I did a Google search on "startup roadmap" and wasn't satisfied with what I found, so I created my own high-level Startup Execution Roadmap along with a more detailed Startup Execution Blueprint. (Both are free downloads on my website: *www.FundableStartups.com*) I use both of these resources to guide my work when I coach and advise startups.

Without a roadmap, any guidance resembles art more than science. Eric Ries writes in his best-selling book *The Lean Startup* that "startup success can be engineered by following the right process, which means it can be learned, which means it can be taught." Following a process reduces the art and increases the science in the equation. Failing to use a methodical process in the form of a roadmap or framework usually results in random, uncoordinated improvements that fail to deliver systematic, tangible, and substantive results. It does little good to have eleven players on a football team randomly run across the field. To beat a challenging opponent, the players each play a specific position and have specific responsibilities. When each player correctly executes the play in the playbook, success is more likely.

"Startup success can be engineered by following the right process."

~ *Eric Ries*, The Lean Startup

Nancy provides solid processes and frameworks to guide a team at play. These processes serve as recipes to properly plan meetings so advisors are well-prepared and not asked to give spontaneous advice. They also help ensure that there's a regular cadence to meetings between the advisor and the company.

Tools

The third element of a business operation or function is tools. Most hard problems are not solved by just talking about what the issues are and why they are important. Problems are more likely to be addressed when the discussion includes details on how to implement a solution. It's the difference between informing a company versus truly transforming it. Tools are key to the transformation, as they increase speed, improve quality, and create consistency while also decreasing time and costs required. Good tools can also enable less experienced individuals to produce results similar to a highly skilled craftsman.

I saw this difference in outcomes first-hand when I needed two doors replaced in a rental home. The tenant was a tradesman (an electrician) and decided to do the work himself. He spent several hours trying to drill the holes in the right place and properly attach the hinges. When he finally mounted the door, it was misaligned and didn't close correctly. We ended up throwing away the door and abandoning his work. I then hired a professional door installer who showed up with several purpose-built, precision jigs that allowed him to quickly and perfectly cut the holes, install the hinges, and mount two doors in half the time it took the electrician's tools to ruin one door.

Nancy's generosity in sharing some ready-to-use tools and templates to simplify tasks, such as assembling an advisory team, planning the work, and implementing real-world changes, is illuminating. She has provided the inquiring entrepreneur with methods to support their vision. This deeply enhances the security around moving forward with the right team and plans.

Plans

Every athlete or competitor should make a game plan. Sun Tzu writes in his seminal work *The Art of War* that "every battle is won before it is ever fought." Great game plans enable weaker teams to beat stronger opponents. One of the best examples is the "master plan" that coach Herb Brooks developed that powered the 1980 U. S. Olympic ice hockey team to victory over the heavily favored, stronger, and more experienced team from the Soviet Union.

> *"Every battle is won before it is ever fought."*
> ~ Sun Tzu, The Art of War

The Soviets had won the previous four Olympic gold medals and 12 of the 16 prior world championships. The Soviet team also won all 12 matches against the US from 1960 to 1980, outscoring the Americans by a blistering 117-26 margin. In fact, just one week before the Olympic Games, the Soviets crushed the American team by a score of 10-3. The Americans fielded a team of unknown, amateur college-level players. The Soviet team was stacked with veteran players with years of professional experience. The average age of the American team was 22 compared to 26 for the Soviets. No one expected the American team to beat the powerhouse Soviet team. But beat them they did in the "Miracle on Ice," which many consider to be one of the greatest upsets in sports history. The American team would go on to win Olympic gold. The Soviet team was so disappointed that they abandoned tradition and refused to have their names engraved on the back of their silver medals. All this was possible because the US coach developed a great game plan and trained his team to execute it to perfection.

> *"The thing that has stuck in my mind all these years is the brilliance of Herb and his master plan."*
> ~ Craig Patrick, Team USA's assistant coach and Hockey Hall of Famer

Nancy's "Advisory Board Builder" and "The Ultimate Board Meeting Blueprint" provide exceptional foundations for leaders to build strong plans that invoke tangible outcomes with real benefits. If you engage with Nancy's strategies, you'll get to play and win with your best abilities. You'll have a safe plan for reference.

In Conclusion

No one sets out to fail at their vision, yet too many people do. I believe that leaders who assemble the right people, follow the right processes, use the right tools, and build the right plan can create a powerful asset — a game-changing advisory board. Thankfully, Nancy provides a great resource to help you do just that.

About Sam Wong

Sam is a startup CEO coach, interim CEO/CTO/CFO, a Silicon Valley advisor and the author of *21 Secrets of Successful Startups*, a book about world-class execution for startups. Sam also provides online training for entrepreneurs at *www.FundableStartups.com*. As a serial entrepreneur, he has been CEO, CTO, or VP Engineering / TechOps for five companies, driving multiple acquisitions as large as $125M. Sam is a popular conference speaker and is widely recognized as a leader in creating insightful, deep-dive, actionable content for startups.

AUTHOR'S NOTE

"Knowledge itself is power"— a meaningful phrase, most likely coined by Sir Francis Bacon. I agree. Power Play Profit Solutions has succeeded upon my principles of helping my clients make knowledgeable decisions. I have coupled power with play. Why? The benefit of play is under continuing scientific study for its powerful magnification of our learning abilities. It ignites the prefrontal cortex, which elevates clear thought. Play also happens to be my favorite pastime, so why not bring this fun, effective tool that magnifies our power into work?

Alongside my career championing and co-creating successes, I have been a voracious learner. Give me knowledge, and I will consume it. Give me experiences, and I will have them. These are the ingredients of smart play.

So how does one obsessed with play decide to focus on, facilitate, and create foundations for running successful advisory boards? In my case, I employed my opportunistic nature to put my Power Play principles to the test to strategize and design practices to make this tool shine.

But where did I first meet advisory boards? This tool was presented at an innovation games summit where I was presenting. The buzz that year was on CABs — customer advisory boards. Open to new models of growth creation for clients, I intuitively leaned in. The speaker announced, "To execute a customer advisory board successfully, you need someone who is an innovation games facilitator" (I was) and "event manager" (score!).

I pivoted my business model to become the customer advisory board specialist for small- to medium-sized tech companies. The market was under-served. I was uniquely qualified to help support its development based on my work history and interests. Woo-hoo!

Research led me through the facts, stats, and practices of advisory boards.

Only six percent of companies were making use of them yet most of those companies had three times revenue increase and double productivity, significantly impacting profitability. We often dream of a secret business tool to make us into what we envision. To me, this was becoming it.

Once my basic advisory board package was presentable, I took it as my offering to conferences. My intention was some upfront assessment of this lopsided statistic. With such high success statistics, why were so few companies using or gaining from it? It became clear. Very few people had grasped the nuances of an advisory board. Some had never heard of them and jumped to the myth I dispel that they are anything like the regulated board of directors we're used to and limited by. Some sat on an advisory board, yet when they described their practices, players, and procedures, my gut said that their team was not working to its most powerful and playful capacity.

To create the *Advisory Board Playbook* I went to work in much the manner that is reflected in this guide itself. I combined my own unique expertise to create this blueprint and pass on my knowledge. To create an advisory board, one is assembling all the best expertise of people and passing on their knowledge to support their vision.

Exert with play, and advance with power.

INTRODUCTION

If someone told you that you could have six to eight of the most successful people you know helping you solve your biggest business challenges, and that they would be honored and delighted to do so, how would you feel? Does that sound too good to be true? It's not. It's an advisory board.

An advisory board is a group of powerful business players working collaboratively in a safe and formalized setting to help your business grow. Tapping into an advisory board's wealth of knowledge unleashes benefits that include compressed timelines as well as increases in revenue, productivity, and valuation. Add to that a collective team wisdom actively decreasing the costly mistakes of an average career span. All together, there are hundreds of thousands — sometimes millions — of dollars available for saving.

Only a tiny percentage of business owners have already adopted this age-old technique. By embracing the information in this book, you'll be part of that small elite group. You'll take businesses to the next level earlier in your career and more safely than a historically low-level of advisory boards in business development has allowed. And it's a tool for excelling a community or peer group, as well.

We all need advice. Working with mentors and coaches is an excellent way to receive tips and tricks, but is a one-on-one experience. The six-to-eight person advisory board steered toward profitable solutions and innovative ideas by a professional facilitator multiplies the mentorship effect, strategically and thoughtfully.

Let's do the arithmetic. You might spend two to three hours at a time with one mentor, multiplied by the number of mentor conversations and benefit from one person's experience. An advisory board gives you the benefit of several minds, and their area of expertise, helping you create more innovative ideas in the same amount of time or less.

One of the biggest advantages of an advisory board is the opportunity to build relational capital and increase your circle of influence. Your advisors might bring their suitable contacts to you just as you will to them. Thus, your relationship with your advisors will also be elevated by the quality of the other people committed to helping your company.

Feeling shy about entrusting a board and can't quite figure out your hesitancy? Perhaps you're experiencing the most common misunderstanding I found amongst the community while making this career shift: mistaking an advisory board for a board of directors. A board of directors has its function, but it also has downfalls an advisory board doesn't have.

Since I believe in a playful and powerful life where success is ignited by innovation and collaboration, I opted for a more interactive-type of board as my niche. In fact, there are many different types of advisory boards, which we will deep dive into in this book. Advisory boards offer a desired approach to collaborative working. The process of supporting the entrepreneur is enjoyable and beneficial for all involved.

This book will

- outline the benefits of an advisory board;
- provide a step-by-step guide to setting up an advisory board;
- supply professional facilitation tools and techniques to ensure you create impactful, productive, and fun advisory board meetings; and
- educate you about the four types of advisory boards and when to implement them.

By following the principles in this book, you will learn to

- arrive at the necessary outcomes to level-up your business;
- ensure the best solutions to pressing problems;

- get advisor experience to shape and develop decision-making abilities that will save money and time, as well as eliminate costly mistakes;
- learn from world-class advisors' stories embedded within to illuminate material; and
- develop a lean mentality and learn to ideate and validate before you execute.

By the end of this book you'll understand how to set up and run an incredible board of advisors. You'll know the best players to get on your team for expertise, advice, and connection.

You'll have the skills to

- direct, organize, and lead the board of advisors;
- make the most of your time with them (in person and follow-up);
- run a high-level meeting that is engaging, fun, and productive; and
- use advisor guidance to leverage both your internal and external communications.

The four types of advisory boards that are the focus of this book include: strategic, customer, community, and peer. You'll discover the right board for your purposes and see how the skills, strategies, and information provided work uniquely for each.

Each type of board leads to a different business outcome.

- Strategic boards develop a business road map.
- Customer advisory boards develop product road maps.
- Community boards maximize contributions.
- Peer advisory boards give and provide support in reciprocity with each member.

This book is in four parts for easy navigation. If you're completely new to the concept of an advisory board, start with Part 1 and work forward. If you're in familiar territory, jump around and learn from the relevant sections.

From recruiting, follow-up, and continuity tips to professional facilitation, Power Play Profit Solutions has put together this book to ensure a completely satisfactory process for both entrepreneurs and advisory board members. These are the tools to foster a web of benefits for everyone involved.

PART ONE

THE CASE FOR ADVISORY BOARDS

> "The best advice I ever got was that knowledge is power and to keep reading."
>
> ~ David Bailey

Section I
POWER

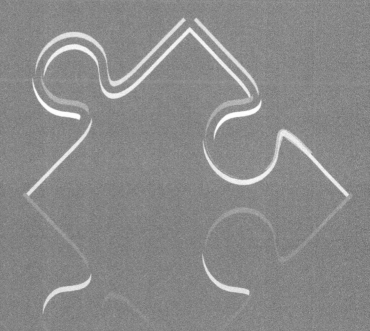

THE POWER OF THE ADVISORY BOARD

When considering a business decision, have you ever wished you could bounce your ideas off someone? An advisory board gives you this opportunity, helping you validate your ideas and focus on the best solutions.

In today's business environment, collaboration and innovation are keys to success. You cannot know everything; in fact, you don't know what you don't know. Creating a collaborative network of successful business owners, and using them to help you create innovative ideas, will give you a competitive advantage. If you do this right, you walk away with the information that will upgrade the way you fundamentally do business.

Unfortunately, fear often stops people from reaching out to advisors and using this incredible business building tool.

Do you recognize any of these most common concerns when it comes to asking for help?

- People will tell me what to do and I may not like their advice.
- An advisory board will cost a lot.
- I'm not prepared to engage, open up, and grow.
- I will have to share the underbelly of problems my business is experiencing.
- The people I ask to be advisors will say "no."

Allowing these prevailing fears denies business owners access to exponential growth. It robs potential advisors of the feeling of giving and receiving if positions are never created for them. Learning about the power of advisory boards is the best cure.

The world is full of successful business people who want to pay forward the riches of their knowledge and experience. You simply need to be brave enough to ask and watch as the helping hands extend themselves in your direction. Ultra successful people want to give back, albeit in a structured and formalized way that will limit their time commitment and maximize the value they can bring to the table.

As your advisors see you implement their advice, their vested interest will grow and they will return to your table with more each time. Business owners have received funding, and more, from listening to their board.

Based on a research study done by the Business Development Bank of Canada (BDC), less than 6% of Small to Medium Enterprises (SMEs) currently use a formalized advisory board. On average, that 6% have tripled their sales and doubled their productivity. This is exactly the same result shown by a previous study done in the U.S. ten years earlier. If only 6% are asking, the untapped pool of advice givers is huge. The advisory board model returns a high level of coaching for a relatively low investment.

"You are the average of the five people you spend the most time with."

~ *Jim Rohn*

Success through association is a great driver in life. Your relationships can make or break you, and so you want to establish powerful, authentic, and effective ones. The power in these connections will accelerate your growth through the association with known and successful people.

ADVICE FROM THE ADVISORS

How to Expand your Circle of Influence

1) Be a person of value — be relevant and look, talk, and think value.

2) You want the favor of conversation — be a person people want to meet, and act so that they speak well of you.

3) Write articles and do interviews — nurture and respect all relationships.

4) Join organizations and foundations.

5) Be known, liked, and trusted …

6) Become the best person you can be.

~ Dr. Nido Qubein

What is an Advisory Board?

A great advisory board is a carefully chosen collective of power players designed to expand your business. It is ideally a group of six to eight people with a vested interest in helping to take your business to the next level.

Their role is to provide business advice and create an environment where your leadership team receives guidance and has a sense of accountability. By bringing a wide variety of experience, they can help you eliminate costly mistakes and bring ideas you may not have found on your own. It often involves an opportunity for board members to gain connections and introductions outside their current network.

Boards can be designed to achieve 3 key purposes:
- Advice • Access • Funds

An advisory board is guaranteed to
- Make money • Save time • Expand networks

Advisory boards can be segmented into at least four categories for four different purposes. The four boards included in this program are:

1. **Strategic:** make better decisions
2. **Customer:** get valuable product feedback
3. **Community:** support a cause and make things happen
4. **Peer:** obtain accountability and support

Putting together an advisory board is work. In fact, it could take up to 100 hours of your time to do it correctly. It is a commitment that will yield great results.

As a proactive business leader, you can assemble your own advisory board, reducing costs and achieving insightful outcomes to accelerate business growth. Assembling such a group generates collaborative ideas and innovative solutions. This board will keep your business focused and strategically ahead of the game.

Board of Directors

A board of advisors is absolutely not the same thing as a board of directors. People often confuse the two. As a result, companies and entrepreneurs shy away from exploring an advisory board, missing its value and power.

A board of directors tends to be part of a large corporation, its central purpose to protect the interests of shareholders. They are formal and can be expensive. When a business incorporates, its minute books are required to include information on its board of directors, but other than that most companies do not set up any functional type of board.

Unlike the board of directors, the advisory board does not have the authority to vote on corporate matters or bear legal fiduciary responsibilities. By understanding some responsibilities of advisory board members, you'll be comfortable moving forward in the process. Please keep in mind that the responsibilities will depend on the type of advisory board you choose, as well as the requirements of your organization.

By understanding some responsibilities of advisory board members, you'll be comfortable moving forward in the process. Please keep in mind that the responsibilities will depend on the type of advisory board you choose, as well as the requirements of your organization.

> *Key distinction: The B.O.D. can fire the CEO on behalf of shareholders. An advisory board supports the business owner.*

Responsibilities of Advisory Board Members

- Provide an independent source of expertise on business, market, and industry trends
- Act as a resource to provide experience-based insights and ideas from an outside perspective
- Participate in critical conversations and collaborate on creating innovative solutions for some of the challenges the business is experiencing
- Help the management team prototype and explore new business ideas
- Act as a sounding board for the management team and a source for contacts
- Help develop frameworks and systems that lead to growth and greater profitability
- Monitor performance and challenge the management team to implement strategies to improve the business structures
- Establish action plans and hold the management team accountable
- Provide a social networking opportunity for the members and the management team that will increase the company's sphere of influence

ADVICE FROM THE ADVISORS

Advisory boards are relatively new. I wish I knew more about them and had advisors to help me over the rough spots — what to look out for if you were in a financial or other business situation. To have access to someone who has the knowledge and information — I wish I had it sooner. Picking out the right advisor is critical to the success of any company. Get the best person and the right person to the right job.

~ George Ross

The Power of Collective Thinking

"Many ideas grow better when transplanted into another mind than the one where they sprang up."

~ Oliver Wendell Holmes

Ideas and solutions grow exponentially when they are shared within a group. The mind performs best with relationships that enable trust. A business performs better with an expert collective. Advisors are helpful for brainstorming, identifying obstacles, and co-creating solutions. They offer an ear to confide in when you're alone at the top of an organization. They've been there. The benefit of a collective is that when your unique group meets it will create another entity that is greater than the sum of its parts.

One well-known form of collective advice is the mastermind principle.

> **The Mastermind principle consists of an alliance of two or more minds working in perfect harmony for the attainment of a common objective.**
>
> **No two minds can ever come together without a third invisible force, which may be likened to a "third mind." When a group of individual minds are coordinated and function in harmony, the increased energy created through that alliance becomes available to every individual in the group.**
>
> **~ Napoleon Hill, Think and Grow Rich (1937).**

The collective of hand-picked talent directed toward one's business or cause saves precious hours of time often spent in one-on-one scenarios with numerous mentors. A benefit for the participants is that this collective's energy becomes available to every individual in the group. The energy generated then makes its way into the exterior endeavors of the board members. In a sense, it is a gift you are giving to your advisors in return for their help.

The ability to obtain valuable advice that produces a positive business impact is an invaluable leadership skill. It is impossible for one person to have the best knowledge in each situation. If possible, do ask for the advice in a formalized and fun way. The results will change your business.

ADVICE FROM THE ADVISORS

"I bring great people together to have *idea sex*." When people form connections with a goal to help solve a business challenge, the sum of the parts is greater than the whole. It starts with a question like, "What can I do for you?" It is great to give before you ask and to share and bring a gift.

"*Ikigai*" — It is composed of two words: *iki*, which means life, and *gai*, which describes value or worth. It is a Japanese concept that means "a reason for being." The word ikigai is usually used to indicate the source of value in one's life or the things that make one's life worthwhile. For many advisors, this is a reason for being because it answers a passion (something they are good at), a vocation (something the world needs), and a professional need (something that is highly valued)."

~ Brian Crombie

The Power of Association

"Leadership is about making others better as a result of your presence and making sure that impact lasts in your absence."

~ Sheryl Sandberg, COO of Facebook

Reputation is important in business and for a very good reason. Reliability, quality delivery of goods or services, and tangible momentum create faith. The people you consider for your advisory board may have a very good reputation in the business world. Some might be refined shining stars, while others may fly under the wire with smooth sailing skills. All these people have earned their place by powerful game play.

> Having all these great people associated with your company boosts your company value. Outsiders are impressed and will trust in your inside operations more for business-to-business. This is especially valuable for tech startups looking for investment funding.

You've worked very hard from your original vision to your current point of success. Throughout that process, you may have popped onto the radar of some of these key players, just as they would have to their predecessors on the success path. Many business people are looking to give back to their communities now that their own accomplishments are taken care of. They can pass along value to you not only through their advice and nurturing, but also through their reputation.

Having steadfast advisors associated with your business boosts your company value. Reinforce this advantage by adding their names and bios to your website and on key company collateral. In addition, you can call on them to:

- be guest speakers at company gatherings, which provides continued internal motivation for employees;
- speak at annual general meetings, which provides exterior assurance and reinforcement to shareholders;
- offer a third-eye perspective and say the things about you and your business that need to be heard, which provides an outsider's stamp of approval; and
- provide assurance to everyone associated with you — from customers to fellow entrepreneurs — that you are on the right track and your endeavor is worthy of trust and success.

ADVICE FROM THE ADVISORS

When you do ask, understand that these people are very busy so it is important to 1) make sure you are not wasting their time; and 2) stack the group with people who want to be around each other. The main reason I sit on boards is because it gives me the access and time with people who were on the board that I wanted to be around, and it made me more passionate about people's products and services and served a dual purpose.

~ Mitch Joel

The Power of Focus

"Always focus on the front windshield and not the rear view mirror."

~ Colin Powell

How many times have you decided to set aside some time to do some strategic thinking on your own or with your team — and it didn't happen? Or booked a casual lunch with a business acquaintance to pick their brain — and then pushed that plan back months at a time as the day-to-day operations ruthlessly demanded your attention?

Strategic thinking is an important skill set that is critical for running a business. In its simplest form, it is an ability to plan for the future and requires dedicated time to think through what you are building and why. It involves thinking about both the changing environments and the various business challenges your company might face. It also involves being able to validate any assumptions that are made while going through building and revising a strategic plan for your advisory board meeting. This takes time and focus.

Focus:
An advisory board proactively drives your business instead of your business driving you.

A key skill for strategic thinkers is that they always seek advice from others. In preparing for the future and an upcoming advisory board meeting, the founder needs a well defined strategic plan ready and needs to welcome feedback and advice from others. During the meeting, they can test ideas and concepts and ensure that the decisions made are incorporated where relevant. This process makes plans and strategies as robust and steadfast as possible.

Your advisory board will help you set aside guaranteed, distraction-free time to focus on your business's strategic growth, not just its current operations. This is known as working *on* your business. Of course, the people working for you must keep their eyes on the day-to-day operations with you. This is generally known as working *in* your business and this is where most business owners get caught up.

When you set that advisory board meeting, you know that you must be prepared to focus all your time and attention to optimize the time you have with these important players. They are not your employees, available day after day in your office. They are not there to mix and mingle with work life. They are there to help, watch, and nudge you into the results your business deserves.

ADVICE FROM THE ADVISORS

For companies to go from startup to scale-up they need strategy, discipline, and focus. For small- and medium-sized companies to scale-up, based on the advice of their advisors, the key is *radical focus*. When you want to grow fast you have to get on your message and repeat yourself a lot. Growth sucks cash, so you need to focus on things that matter like shortening your cycles, sales, and delivery.

~ Verne Harnish

The Power of Results

"Insanity is doing the same thing over and over again and expecting different results."

~ Albert Einstein

It's as simple as this: the businesses with active advisory boards are the ones getting results because they do things differently. It is essentially a foolproof system that will provide you with good advice from successful people who have been there before. The advice you act upon is proven, increasing the likelihood that you will experience better results. Yet the current user rate of advisory boards is a mere 6% among small- and medium-sized enterprises (SMEs).

> Based on the Business Development Corporation's (BDC) 2014 report, of the 6% of SMEs actively working with advisory boards, the following average increases have been reported:
>
> **3X Increase in Sales**
>
> **2X Increase in Productivity**

The remaining 94% of SMEs who don't currently have advisory boards could experience these increases by adopting this invaluable business tool. Is it worth running your business with only the strategies you knew when you began? You don't know what you don't know.

Advisory boards offer a great R.O.I. Imagine triple sales result from a small percentage investment.

Coincidentally, the number of companies that make it to five years in business is also a very small 6%. That means if you've made it this far, it's time to switch to the other 6% and grow into a permanent success. And if you're in your infancy, consider an advisory board strategy early rather than when you're in danger.

ADVICE FROM THE ADVISORS

An advisor becomes part of a cloud of people, and in the way that we each develop our own business in our own personal cloud, we advisors become one more person discussing you in your absence. Suddenly, we're tossing our talk of your company, your skilled leadership and results, up into this cloud. I do a lot of speaking gigs, for instance. At breakout sessions, around the coffee urn, or at after parties, I get to meet other business leaders who can benefit by the relationship my advisory role with a company provides. And that puts my promotional effort into the ever-widening cloud of the company I advise for.

~ Nolan Bushnell

The Power of Action

"Take time to deliberate; but when the time for action arrives, stop thinking and go in."

~ Andrew Jackson

Your advisory board offers different levels of coaching — a collective process that is simple to implement. This collective process brings together an amazing group of people ready to focus all their expertise, ideas, and connections on bringing your business to new heights and creating visions and pathways to achievement. When you take the right steps, you can step into your success.

You can

- become part of the 6% who are crushing it;
- create an environment where the collective knowledge is focused on solving your challenges;
- gain contacts;
- avoid mistakes;
- generate a collaborative solution that would not have happened in isolation, or even with a one-on-one scenario;
- build trust with business heavyweights;
- open opportunity for these connections to invest since they believe in you; and

- increase your value by having the association with business tycoons on your side.

All sizes of organizations can and do have advisory boards. Typically, a fast-growing company will assemble an advisory board because they have so many critical decisions to make and need the advice of experts who have been there before and are interested in doing the right thing at the right time. However, an advisory board can be applicable to start-ups who have no budget but can benefit from being associated with the right people. When you take action based on world-class expertise you have created a gateway to exponential growth and real success. You aren't left behind wondering if you *should have*.

It's time to give yourself permission to succeed. But if you decide to do this, do it right. The more you learn ahead of time, the more organized you will be, and the better chance you'll have of WOWing your advisors. In turn, their collective power will provide exponential and unprecedented success for you.

ADVICE FROM THE ADVISORS

Ideas are nothing and implementation is everything. The time between the moment you come up with the right strategy to the moment you implement it will determine how successful you are going to be ... strategic thinking in business is as important as breathing; it is the gateway to innovation. A wise man learns from his mistakes while a genius learns from other people's mistakes.

~ JT Foxx

Section II
VALUE

THE VALUE OF AN ADVISOR

What exactly is an advisor, anyway? You've now spent time understanding the invaluable tool of advisory boards. You're ready to consider who to put on your board.

An advisor is a person who has achieved a recognizable expertise in a niche that they can then bring forth as guidance to a budding business person. They might also, after a distinguished career, have multidisciplinary experience to compliment their work on your advisory board. They take a leadership role in your company, and this is to your benefit.

> *Seeking and giving advice are very important for effective leadership and decision making. These are practical skills you can learn and apply to great effect... When the exchange is done well, people on both sides of the table benefit.*
>
> *Those who are truly open to guidance (and not just looking for validation) develop better solutions to problems than they would have on their own. They add nuance and texture to their thinking — and, research shows, they can overcome cognitive biases, self-serving rationales, and other flaws in their logic.*
>
> ~ *David A. Garvin | Joshua D. Margolis,*
> Harvard Business Review, Jan / Feb, 2015,
> https://hbr.org/2015/01/the-art-of-giving-and-receiving-advice

When assembling a team of advisors, you might be tempted to seek out like-minded individuals. In fact, variety is not just the spice of life it is integral to a balanced group of minds that can offer a gamut of perspectives, strategies, and skills. Through this balance, the advisors also gain knowledge from the rest of your advisory board.

Mentor vs Advisor

Mentor = One-on-one

Advisors = Collective

First, pinpoint where you need help, and be honest about the areas that could use your advice. Think about who the industry heavy-weights and talents are, envision who you would want to have on this "dream team," and look at the criteria that makes them the right fit, such as their track record and connections in the operational areas most crucial to your success. As you open your vision beyond what is and into what could be, you'll want to ensure you choose the right advisors.

What Makes a Good Advisor?

 "Always give without remembering and always receive without forgetting."

~ Brian Tracy

A good advisor is someone who

- has experienced success in business;
- understands business, market, and industry trends;
- provides "wise counsel" on issues raised by owners or management;
- is a well-respected leader; and
- cares and is interested in helping others succeed.

Five stages of finding and getting good advice*

1. Find the right fit
    - What knowledge gaps do you need filled?
    - Will they want to help for the right reasons?
2. Develop a shared understanding
    - Work together to clarify the desired outcomes.
3. Craft alternatives
    - Many methods generate many ideas.
4. Converge on a decision
    - Set criteria for taking ideas forward and for selecting solutions for desired results.
5. Put advice into action
    - It is imperative that you do something with the advice you are given otherwise it can do more damage than good to the relationship with an advisor.

---

* Condensed and paraphrased from HBR's full version. "The Art of Giving and Receiving Advice," by David A. Garvin and Joshua D. Margolis, is available online at *Harvard Business Review*, https://hbr.org/2015/01/the-art-of-giving-and-receiving-advice.

Some of the people on your list may be close to your current network and some may be further away. It is very difficult to measure people, as each one comes with myriad skills and talents. Some people's qualities will be right on the surface and some will be less obvious. Consider the first brainstorm of people using the five stages of advising as a helpful tool.

To be responsible for your decision making, you need to be responsible for the creation of a complete business overview of the key metrics of your business. These key metrics include your profitability, your current growth, the key challenges, your business uniqueness, your potential market opportunities, customer feedback on your products and service, your desired level of profitability, markets, and market share (if possible).

This complete business overview should be shared in confidence with your advisors. When you are choosing an advisor you must first and foremost find someone you trust. You will have to be vulnerable and let these hand-picked experts see everything — the good, the bad, and the ugly. They can't help you if they don't know the real story.

Relax. Within the confines of strict confidentiality it should be a stress-free, positive time to look clearly at your business and allow the experts to help you.

ADVICE FROM THE ADVISORS

A coach is a very observant individual who will look at some of the improvements to be made and communicate those improvements and help you achieve them. An advisor will do something different. An advisor will observe, use their own knowledge, provide you with information and yet not do it ... Never use lawyers, accountants, or consultants as advisors — use individuals who are arm's length and have no vested interest, otherwise the advice you get will be tainted.

~ Rony Israel

The Value of Knowledge

"Knowledge is of no value unless you put it into practice."

~ Anton Chekhov

Advising is essentially the sharing of knowledge based on learned and practiced expertise. Your advisory board gives you the benefit of six to eight experienced minds open to deliver their knowledge and aid in implementing a better future for you. Those advisors also benefit in myriad ways, because they all learn new things from each other. They see different approaches to solving a problem which could also be applicable to their own business.

The following, from a January 2015 article in *Harvard Business Review*, are some of the ways advisors can provide knowledge. What you do with it is always up to you. As long as you treat these suggestions with care and consideration, there is a limitless well of perspective and direction you can gather from your advisory board.

What Advisers Can Do
Depending on what's needed, advisers might:

Serve as a sounding board	Test a tentative path	Expand the frame of reference	Provide process guidance	Generate substantive ideas
Restate and play back arguments to sharpen the seeker's understanding of the situation and the conclusions she has drawn	Scrutinize the reasoning behind the selection of an option and elaborate on the potential consequences	Provide greater breadth and depth of understanding about the nature of the problem the seeker faces—and the implications for action	Suggest how to approach and manage a complicated, delicate, or high-stakes situation	Increase the number and range of options being considered

KEY PRACTICES

Asking a few well-chosen questions that probe the seeker's underlying rationale and motivation—and listening attentively	Assessing the seeker's thinking, often using hypotheticals and critical questions to achieve a deeper understanding	Sharing key details and tendencies from prior experiences in similar situations to flesh out the larger context	Examining the interests involved, the possibilities for action, and alternative steps the seeker might take	Brainstorming with the seeker

~ "The Art of Giving and Receiving Advice," David A. Garvin and Joshua D. Margolis, *Harvard Business Review*, https://hbr.org/2015/01/the-art-of-giving-and-receiving-advice.

ADVICE FROM THE ADVISORS

Having advisors when I was first selling one of my companies, I gained a more mature perspective. The acquirer was playing all sorts of tricks and games. My advisors reminded me that is a game (one they had played many times — a multi-dimensional chess) and it wasn't personal, don't get offended or frustrated. Figure out the strategy, gradually move the pieces, and see what opens up. They would see three moves ahead that I couldn't. By listening to my advisors, I got a much better price.

~ Christine Comaford

The Value of Connection

"The business of business is relationships; the business of life is human connection."

~ Robin S. Sharma

Relationships are a driving force of humanity. As people, we continue to evolve and define ourselves through our relationships. Yet, many of us are awkward in this arena.

Consider relationship building skills as an immediate way to level up your day, connections, and career. These soft skills are what a person applies to connect with others. They make room for positivity. In the workplace, relationship building skills are essential for getting along with coworkers, contributing to a team, and building an understanding between yourself and others. When you are expanding your sphere of influence with successful advisors, relationship skills forge clear connections.

Many leaders have failed at the effort required to become emotionally adept, self-aware, and secure enough to avoid the pitfalls of bad relationships. Lacking these skills is becoming increasingly known as a career risk. Play is such a powerful facilitator to healthy power because it challenges us to get better at relating to one another so that we have power together, not power over, even where winning and losing are concerned.

> *Involvement in an advisory board gives people an opportunity to further connections with the things and people they enjoy.*

In the leadership sphere, founders will be wise to preserve time and space for themselves around relationships. This is like a secret magic to life. Healthy relationship and connection dynamics ease the mind and allow work the sanctity it needs. Be authentic with people and they will shine. Show them you're curious, listening, and appreciative to break down barriers with grace. The reward is the good company you've asked for.

Being part of an advisory board gives people the opportunity to create new relationships, to foster existing ones, and to use their relationships to create new connections for other people — such as you. It's a win-win-win, because everyone makes new business connections, and it's a big reason why advisors choose to help out and serve on boards.

Has someone in your circle of influence already expressed interest in helping you out, but you didn't know how to follow through and ask? Does your product or service have a mutual benefit with a potential advisor's business? Do you have an industry connection you have heard speak at conferences, who you know would be excited by the opportunity?

Use your six degrees of separation and find a way to approach someone you know you want to work with. If you were on the other side, wouldn't you appreciate being asked?

ADVICE FROM THE ADVISORS

The value you get out of an advisory board, sometimes it goes beyond what you give to the company; it's those relations you build on the board and I think that that is true and I've experienced that.

~ Jason Morsink

The Value of Commitment

"Individual commitment to a group effort — that is what makes a team work, a company work, a society work, a civilization work."

~ Vince Lombardi

Those who accept a position as one of your advisors are interested in their relationship with you and your business. You must cherish the comfort, care, information, and status of this relationship. You have to honor their commitment and always optimize their time and expertise. It's a serious responsibility, but with it comes great joy. The relationships you nourish during this expansion will bring much happiness to the development and future success of your business. That's value added.

When an advisor says yes and signs a contract, you know that they are committed to helping you out. You will find that some advisors are more active and committed than others. For this reason, it is best to develop a method of tracking contribution to the company's growth. Based on those achievements, milestones and results, advisors then earn their compensation and equity.

You equally need to demonstrate to your advisors that you value their advice. Take action and keep them informed of your progress and successes. When you do well they will feel their commitment and advice was time well invested.

Commitment: do or do not. There is no in-between.

ADVICE FROM THE ADVISORS

Small successes lead to big successes. Great things happen when you decide not to give up and to take things to the next level. What is your strategy to be faster, better, more efficient? There is always a way to do it better ... Business is not a solo game — get joy by helping. The more you give, the more you receive.

~ Hugh Hilton

The Value of Contribution

"When you cease to make a contribution, you begin to die."

Eleanor Roosevelt

Believe it or not, there are people who want to help you. Some have watched you grow, believe in your product or service, and feel they could bring something to the table. Some have never heard of you, but will feel a burst of enthusiasm when you approach them and unveil your business and its upcoming needs. Your company is making a difference, and potential advisors want to make a difference too.

Those who've already fulfilled their goals have more room in their lives to help others experience growth and completion. Their hearts are full of generosity and the immense amount of knowledge it took them to achieve their dreams. They have a lot of light to shed and want to see another star shine. That star is you! Allowing those talented individuals to lend their wisdom to your own connects you to positive business communities and a thriving society.

Changing your mindset from that of a lone wolf who worked diligently to create the business you have now to one taking on an advisory board can be unsettling. Some worry that they will share their business and its personal information only to be misunderstood or misdirected by those who've been brought on board. It is important to understand that when people choose to give back they are coming from a place of support and not judgment. Setting clear expectations and being grateful for the opportunity to work with amazing people will hopefully settle all those fears.

ADVICE FROM THE ADVISORS

Most people will step up to be on an advisory board. They want to give back. You are best to look for community-minded people that have some business experience. Even more valuable than that is the dictum, "don't sell to your network, sell to your networks' network." If people on the advisory board think what I am saying makes sense, they are more likely to recommend you — so you get back too.

~ Bob Gold

The Value of Collaboration

"We cannot solve our problems with the same thinking we used when we created them."

~ Albert Einstein

Increasingly, research validates the benefits of collaboration in business. One definition of collaboration is "two or more people working together towards shared goals." This is the underlying value for all the board members when they get together for the purpose of helping your company. By working as a group they can all learn from one another, and many of the ideas generated will be applicable to their other business ventures.

Collaboration

- moves a company more effectively towards its goals;
- is the lifeblood that lets new ideas thrive;
- brings together different types of specialists and experts, which can give people new ways to think and challenge everyone to consider different directions; and
- is the cornerstone of innovative solutions.

Collaboration Technology

Collaboration is having a big impact on the current workplace. As technology allows more people to work remotely, collaboration platforms such as Sharepoint and Slack make it easier for groups to work together.

These can be integrated into the advisory board program, allowing board members to continue to be involved and provide feedback remotely. Nevertheless, it's important to build your relationships right from the start with a powerful face-to-face meeting.

Check out the logos for some collaboration platform choices:

- Zoho Projects
- Wrike
- LiquidPlanner
- Glip by RingCentral
- Slack
- Asana
- Volerro
- LeanKit
- Podio
- Airtable

ADVICE FROM THE ADVISORS

We are consistently reminded by everyone who runs a customer advisory board that the people who show matter because the collaboration from different segments leads to healthy debates and conversations.

Often, we have the right ideas but the wrong sequencing — the sequencing really does matter for the customer to better represent their needs. Once you start mining a vein of conversation it gets really exciting to see where it will go.

~ Luke Hohmann

PART TWO

ADVISORY BOARD BUILDER (ABB):
A Proprietary 5-P Process

> "What if a president established a Presidential Advisory Board that would meet once every couple of months, bringing together the former presidents for a conference in order to seek their collective wisdom? There is a wealth of experience in the former presidents that generally goes untapped."
>
> ~ Tony Campolo

OVERVIEW

Building an advisory board properly is the key to receiving its full rewards. Be warned. The quality of knowledge it takes to build your advisory board cannot be underestimated, nor can the skills required be imitated.

Companies might claim to do "board building" as part of their repertoire; however, they are often ex-recruiters who will go out and find you members for a fee. Still, other companies provide board meeting facilitation services. Both recruitment and facilitation are integral components, yet insufficient without deeper investigation. In this section we're going to look at the work that has to be done internally to figure out why you want to have an advisory board and what types of topics and knowledge you need to bring to the table for it to be effective and bring a high return on investment (ROI).

The real cost of building and running an advisory board is time. The BDC estimates it will take 100 hours of the owner's time to properly build an advisory board. Though you can hire a company to do some of the work, there will always be significant demand on you, the business owner. Because of this demand, the BDC recommends forming an advisory board only if the following conditions are met:

> *The BDC shares key criteria to keep your investment in an advisory board safer.*

- The business must have a strategic plan — without one they cannot communicate their direction and plans effectively to board members.

- The business must have financials and budgets — without those there is not enough information to evaluate the business health.
- The business must have a management team in place — because so much of the owner's time will be directed to this project that they need good people running the business.

These criteria from the BDC are mostly applicable to a strategic advisory board. ROI on other types of advisory boards will require time and commitment, and we will look at this in more depth in Part 4.

Advisory Board Builder (ABB)

This proprietary approach to your excelled success is called the Advisory Board Builder (ABB). This is the methodology to build the right advisory board for the right reasons, using the right tools and techniques to have a rewarding experience for everyone involved. Each part of the ABB process incorporates a variety of techniques that will help you generate the results you need.

Outcomes of the 5-P Process:

1) **Purpose:** Determine your board's purpose(s) and outcomes
   - advice, funding, access
2) **Players:** Identify and recruit your power players
   - experience, expertise, connections
3) **Preparation:** Lead and direct the board
   - provide laser focus for board members
4) **Planning:** Plan and run ultra-productive meetings
   - leverage the minds and networks of members to achieve the board's objectives
5) **Performance:** Implement and update
   - output into action, with updates that cause board members to feel heard, heeded, and trusted

---

5-P PROCESS

1) Purpose

There are different ways to assess the kind of advice that you need. For instance, a blend of in-depth questionnaires, analysis models, and an understanding of your organization's topics or challenges in the next 12–18 months, combined with expert guidance, exposes your purpose. This sets the requirements of the advisory board and determines the types of skills categories that best serve the organization.

5-Ps of the ABB Process:
1) Purpose
2) Players
3) Preparation
4) Planning
5) Performance

2) Players

Based on required skills and knowledge, we identify and select the right members for your team. Then, we recruit and onboard. The book also provides scripts, templates and marketing materials to influence the acceptance of the people you want and help guarantee their commitment.

3) Preparation

Once you have the right people on board for the right reasons, you have to prepare them for the scheduled meeting. Provide relevant information prior to the meeting to provide time to think about your challenges. For example, you might create a shared place for accessing key data on a timely basis or a quick survey for feedback.

They'll need information about the meeting location, time, and agenda. Again, the more you manage your advisors' expectations, respect their time, and ensure they know the details, the more professional and results oriented your big meeting will be.

4) Planning

Planning is the secret to hosting a successful advisory board meeting. An agenda based on relevant topics to be discussed, together with interactive exercises, will give every person an opportunity to contribute and co-create innovative solutions. Based on the desired outcomes, you will reverse engineer your meetings using a variety of traditional and cutting-edge facilitation tools and techniques. This level of professional facilitation will help to ensure the desired outcomes are accurately captured and actionable results come out of the meeting.

5) Performance

Once you have received all sorts of high-value ideas and solutions, you have to make them happen. You need to keep advisory board members informed of the progress the company is making and set performance criteria that will show members you are acting on the advice given. Once an advisor has a vested interest and an active role in helping with the direction and success of your company, developments often supersede initial expectations. Advisors have been known to bring funding to companies or actively coach departments. The surprises an individual can bring vary. Often, the gifts they return to you reflect the value you've made them feel through your implementation of their solutions.

Part of maximizing the performance to an advisory board is creating a communications and reporting program to keep your advisors in the loop. In addition, strategies and product roadmap developments can also be integrated into both internal and external communications. Particularly with startups, promoting your board of advisors can boost the value of the organization by association.

1) PURPOSE

Determine your Board's Purpose(s) and Outcomes

Now that you know how powerful and valuable an advisory board is, you can begin the process of choosing the right kind for your business. Know your options!

The four types of advisory boards this book will cover are:

- Strategic advisory board
- Customer advisory board (CAB)
- Community advisory board
- Peer advisory board

Within each type you will need to have clarity on the desired outcomes for your advisory board. You can answer by determining what kind of advice, service, or feedback would help your organization grow. Ask some questions of yourself to help you figure it out.

- Do you need successful business people to help you make a strategic business decision or solve a pressing challenge that you have not been able to do yourself?
- Do you need your best customers to tell you what they really want and what is working or not working?
- Do you say you're being customer-centric? If so, when is the last time you spoke to your customer?
- Do you need financing as a startup?
- Do you need funding as a not-for-profit and could you also use committed volunteers to help your charity grow?
- Do you need a collaborative opportunity with key peers to support one another's growth?

> These three key criteria have proven the strongest areas of need and are therefore beneficial to figuring out the purpose and type of board people should build:
>
> • *Advice* • *Access* • *Funds*

Advice: WHERE ARE YOUR KNOWLEDGE GAPS?

▶ financial, marketing, operations ...

Access: WHERE ARE YOUR CONTACT AND INFLUENCE GAPS?

▶ to new markets, key suppliers, government ...

Funding: WHERE ARE YOUR FINANCIAL EXPERTISE GAPS?

▶ seed, IPO ...

Is there a combination of different gaps that need to be filled?

ABB Approach

Let me now walk you through my proven methods for determining the purpose of your advisory board(s). I recommend you start to map out each area using a visual tool. It is important to get ideas out of your head and onto the wall so that the team can have a shared understanding and a shared language.

> STEP 1: Gather your best people together because you want to figure out what you need and brainstorm in the three key areas of advice, access, and funding. This is the process to determine your knowledge gaps and find your purpose.

Advice

How do you best go about discovering your knowledge gaps? A great starting point is a SWOT analysis. SWOT stands for:

- Strengths
- Weakness
- Opportunities
- Threats

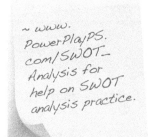

~ www.PowerPlayPS.com/SWOT-Analysis for help on SWOT analysis practice.

To prepare for this exercise, you can send out a short questionnaire to your staff and key stakeholders. Keep to very simple open-ended questions, such as:

▶ What do we do well?
▶ Where could we improve?
▶ What opportunities do you see?
▶ Where are some of the threats that we need to watch out for?

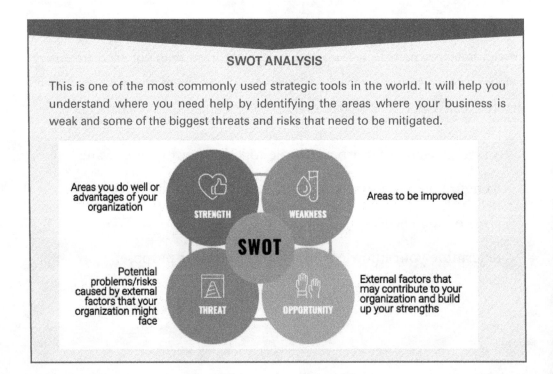

SWOT ANALYSIS

This is one of the most commonly used strategic tools in the world. It will help you understand where you need help by identifying the areas where your business is weak and some of the biggest threats and risks that need to be mitigated.

- **STRENGTH**: Areas you do well or advantages of your organization
- **WEAKNESS**: Areas to be improved
- **THREAT**: Potential problems/risks caused by external factors that your organization might face
- **OPPORTUNITY**: External factors that may contribute to your organization and build up your strengths

DERI LLEWELLYNN DAVIES' 8-BOX SWOT

In his book BGI Strategy On A Page, Deri Llewellyn Davies, known as "the Strategy Guy" in the UK, discusses an eight-box SWOT. It starts with the typical four strategy-based categories: Strengths, Weaknesses, Opportunities, and Threats. Based on where these intersect, Deri has developed the sorts of strategies that will best address the needs of a company. This model helps penetrate and expand the SWOT, with some remedies that will lead to a better understanding of what needs to be done, thereby helping to identify the type of advice that would be beneficial. Already we're getting somewhere in our thinking!

	Strengths	Weaknesses
Opportunities	Wealth Strategy	Development Strategy
Threats	Toughen Up Strategy	Critical Strategy

~ Deri Llewellyn Davies, BGI Strategy on a Page

Above Graph
Wealth Strategy = strengths meet opportunities
Development Strategy = weaknesses meet opportunities
Toughen-up Strategy = strengths meet threats
Critical Strategy = weaknesses meet threats

~ www.BGIStrategy.com

You have to start by understanding where you are before you can begin to envision where you want to be in the future and all the steps to get you there. Based on strengths and weaknesses, begin to build the categories in which you need advice. For example, if you are looking for strategic help, begin by looking at the core strategic areas in any organization. Most commonly, there are six key strategic areas:

- Marketing
- Sales
- Operations
- Finance
- People / HR
- Technology

It doesn't end there. Like a little domino effect of analysis, your industry or business' specialty will lead to your personalized sub-categories. Because you are using this to identify the type of skills that would best meet your challenge, you can be even more specific about the type of skill and knowledge required. For example, marketing splits into digital marketing and traditional marketing, both of which can be further broken down. For example, digital marketing could be broken down into SEO, lead generation, and content creation, whereas marketing could be broken down into publicity, advertising, and branding.

Access

What type of markets do you need to break into to get to the next level?

Again with a group brainstorming session, begin to look at your strengths and weaknesses with respect to contacts. Start by creating access categories that would help. Consider that these might break down further into sub-categories. It could be by industry, by association, by supplier, by government agency, by retailer, or by channel.

Who are the key decision makers who would have a positive impact on the company? Do these decision makers make up a category to consider adding to the list of skills or knowledge that would help the company?

Funding

What type of financial help does your organization need?

Not all companies need funding, and this evaluation criteria is more targeted to a startup or a not-for-profit, where funding is paramount to moving the organization to the next level. What are the skills and knowledge needed to obtain funding from government sources, venture capitalists, Angel Investors, institutions, or donors? Each one needs a different professional approach. Risks and rewards vary by option.

STEP 2: Visualize these requirements by building an *advice board*. Begin by mapping out the key areas. Use large Post-it™ notes for this, and set them up horizontally across the top.

ADVISORY BOARD "WAR ROOM" SET-UP								
PURPOSE STATEMENT			Advice / Access / Funding					
CATEGORY #1	CATEGORY #2	CATEGORY #3	CATEGORY #4	CATEGORY #5	CATEGORY #6	CATEGORY #7	CATEGORY #8	
Candidate #1	Candidate #1	Candidate #1	Candidate #1	Candidate #1	Candidate #1	Candidate #1	Candidate #1	
Candidate #2	Candidate #2	Candidate #2	Candidate #2	Candidate #2	Candidate #2	Candidate #2	Candidate #2	
Candidate #3	Candidate #3	Candidate #3	Candidate #3	Candidate #3	Candidate #3	Candidate #3	Candidate #3	
Candidate #4	Candidate #4	Candidate #4	Candidate #4	Candidate #4	Candidate #4	Candidate #4	Candidate #4	
Candidate #5	Candidate #5	Candidate #5	Candidate #5	Candidate #5	Candidate #5	Candidate #5	Candidate #5	
Candidate #6 Expertise ___ Experience ___ Contacts ___	Candidate #6 Expertise ___ Experience ___ Contacts ___	Candidate #6 Expertise ___ Experience ___ Contacts ___	Candidate #6 Expertise ___ Experience ___ Contacts ___	Candidate #6 Expertise ___ Experience ___ Contacts ___	Candidate #6 Expertise ___ Experience ___ Contacts ___	Candidate #6 Expertise ___ Experience ___ Contacts ___	Candidate #6 Expertise ___ Experience ___ Contacts ___	

You can look at this exercise from a horizontal level, which means setting up the categories horizontally and coming up with as many categories as needed on a high level. As we showed above, it is also valuable to dig a little deeper into each category or topic and keep asking how a category can be broken down on a vertical level.

> Visual tools are your best friend when it comes to categories upon categories. Choose eight categories, write one per sticky note, and line the notes vertically on a wall or portable board. This is the starting point for the next process – choosing your players.

Once you have generated all the different categories you could need, it is time to choose the top eight knowledge gaps you want to fill. First, review all the categories you have established in context of the strategic objectives and prioritize them.

Ask yourself these questions:

- What will drive the highest value for the company?
- Where do we have the biggest gaps?
- Which categories will help address the company's biggest challenges?

You can choose to have the management team vote on which categories address these questions. If there are ties, this is a great opportunity to have some discussions on what the company needs most. You want to choose between six and eight categories. In the end, you will have one advisor for each category.

"More than 8, no collaborate."
~ Luke Hohmann, Innovation Games / Conteneo

You know now what type of advisors to invite to your board, at least in the categorical sense.

2) PLAYERS

Identify your Power Players and Get them on Board

In Step 1, Purpose, you identified the gaps to be filled. In this step, you'll identify the people who can best help the company in each selected category. This is where you become really clear about the kind of person who would best fit for your advisory board.

Who are the people within your current sphere of influence who could fill the gaps? Start there. Then, go beyond people you know. It's time to start dreaming about who you would love to have help advise your business!

Visualize it! Take the eight categories you identified and put them along the top to form a row. Get out more post-it notes and brainstorm again. This brainstorm is all about *who you know* and *who you want* who has expertise to fill in gaps your process has identified. Who might meet those criteria? Envision them.

---

3 steps to identify potential advisors

• Brainstorm   • Evaluate   • Prioritize

The 3 key areas to consider when thinking about your advisors

• Experience   • Expertise   • Connections

Brainstorm

Brainstorming is a great way to generate lots of ideas about who will be on your advisory board. Together with your partners or management team, take some time to generate a list of potential advisors. Include any and all the people who meet the criteria within a category. For instance, if you need digital marketing help, generate names of everyone you know who is good at digital marketing. Even if someone seems far-fetched and the thought of approaching them intimidates you, write that person's name on a sticky and put it under the appropriate category.

In this process, ask for the moon! Consider high-level successful people. Think about the thriving people you know or who are one or two degrees of separation away. If you have a board of directors or a couple of key mentors, invite them to this process, because they can identify even more people within their networks. Aim for a minimum of six names per category.

Every single entrepreneur has at least eight to ten successful associates in their network who are interested in the business and would love to help. It's only a matter of giving them a chance — that's what your advisory board will do!

Evaluate

It's now time to evaluate, in context, what the company needs and the board's purpose. Say you have five or six people in each category who interest you. For the purpose of ranking potential candidates, it is important to think about any relationship already in place. There is an important line between respecting someone and having a professional relationship with them versus asking people who are close friends because you know they will help. Be sure that they are the best fit for the position not the easiest person to invite.

Be warned that it is very important not to have any type of professional services associates or consultants that you are already paying on your advisory board. They may not be able to give you truly objective insights, as some of their ideas will be biased. This means you do not include your accountant or your lawyer. Use discernment with consultants as they may have ulterior motives.

Get judgy! It's time to evaluate and rank these folks based on all the value they bring to the table. I suggest using a scoring system that will help you prioritize the best candidates. Here's how that might look.

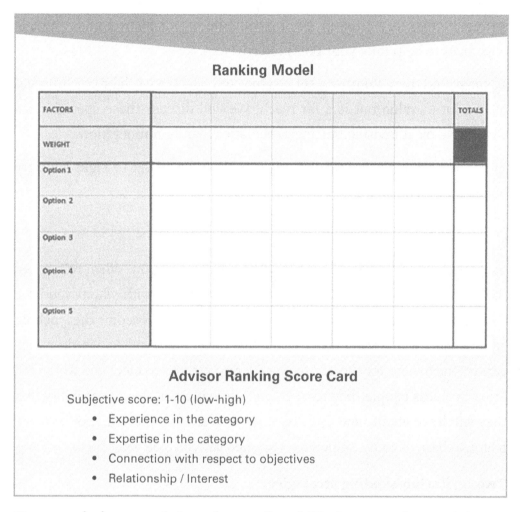

You want the best people in each area of need. The best must be, at minimum, someone who has more success in the area of need than you do right now. They can impart the wisdoms from that success.

A pre-existing relationship or mutual interest may increase the likelihood of their joining your advisory board. There are people already near you who can offer suggestions at this stage. Current employees, a board of directors, mentors, or anyone else who may have good suggestions are helpful in evaluating your potential advisors.

Prioritization

Now that your list is bursting at the seams with potential, you'll have to prioritize. Put the players in order of preference based on the evaluation scores. If there is a toss-up, think about the bigger picture and strategic objectives to help rank your potential advisors.

You may find there is either a subject matter expert or a celebrity who could offer a lot of value but is a far reach. We will discuss these special cases when we look at inviting, setting expectations, and remuneration.

You now have a prioritized list of candidates for all six to eight advisory board positions.

INVITATION AND RECRUITMENT

You'll use your prioritized list to send letters of invitation. When rolling out the invitations, go after the highest profile candidate with whom you have the greatest connection first. One of these people could become the lynchpin advisor who will help you get other high-level advisors. As we discussed earlier, one benefit for the advisors is the opportunity to meet and work with other business people they respect, and there is a very high probability that they will learn about new deals because they are together on your advisory board. Tell them your compelling story, and say why you want them.

Two invitation-sending strategies

Strategy #1

Send one invitation to the number one person in each of your six to eight categories. If the number one choice does not accept the invitation, then move to the number two person per category. Continue down your list until you secure someone for that particular category. If a candidate does not accept, you can ask them if there is anyone else with a similar background and reputation they could recommend.

Strategy #2

Send one to three invitations to heavy-hitters, those people who are well known and could become that lynchpin because of their favorable reputation. You can use their participation as board members to entice prioritized names from your other categories.

Three ways to approach a potential advisor

1) In Person

You may want to take an in-person approach to recruit an advisor or two, armed with collateral, and a will to do whatever it takes to meet that person. This is costlier than the other invitation approaches we'll walk through, but if your gut says "yes" to catch the big fish — and you strike as the professional and not the predator — it will pay off if that person says yes.

2) Personal Call

This is the most effective way to ask someone you respect and admire to be on your advisory board, and also the most difficult. As with any approach, you need to be prepared. You must have done the research on the person and rehearsed the script you will follow once you pick up the phone.

That script will help answer the following questions:

- Why them? Their accomplishments and reputation are worth retelling.
- Why you? Have a compelling story about your company that will inspire them.
- Why now? Let them know about your needs and the key topics you will be addressing.
- Who else? If you have any of your lynchpins signed on, let the other potential advisors know.
- What do you need? Be able to tell them all the details of how much time you are asking from them and what their expectations should be from your organization.

> When making an invitation, by phone or by letter, the three key elements to address are:
>
> • Why them? • Why you? • What to expect!

3) Letter of Invitation

The art of writing a good letter is a priceless skill. Describe a dream that the people you're contacting would want to be associated with. With the right description, the right matches will want to make this dream a reality. It helps to thoroughly research your candidates so that you can demonstrate you've put true thought and care into asking them to be part of your future.

Remember, if you don't ask, you don't know!

You have an idea of who they are and believe there could be a real spark of mutual benefit. Make them feel important because they are.

Whether it be the in-person, the personal call, or the letter of invitation, whichever one of these techniques suits you best, your potential advisors need lots of reasons to want to be part of your team. Find your personal invitation style and make an impression.

PACKAGE

With any of these approaches, you must have a professional package to get into their hands. This should not be done by email, but rather by courier.

Pitch Package

Letter

- Express respect and admiration
- State your purpose: Why them? Why you?
- Indicate the expected time commitment:
    - meeting frequency and location
    - intermittent correspondence
- Benefits: connections, gifts, payment, honorarium, contribution

Company Overview

- Invitation Pitch Deck
    - We recommend using a short and powerful "Pitch Deck" which will answer key questions about your company such as Problem / Solution, Opportunity, Management Team, Strategy
    - Include extras: brochures, website, company collateral material with personal highlights

R.S.V.P.

- Include an acceptable date that allows continuous flow in your recruitment process

DETERMINE EXPECTATIONS

What are your expectations of your board members?

A big part of the decision to work with you comes from your clarity of expectations, as stated for being part of the board. Highlight the number of expected meetings — both in person and online — the length of the meetings, and an approximate length of time required for preparation.

These future advisors will be helping because they are heart-oriented and feel good about being involved. Make your invitation compelling.

Depending on the type of advisory board, you may also want to stipulate expectations for working on committees or funding. Community advisory boards, for example, have more active members who contribute both more time and money. Peer advisory boards are a commitment to one another that require accountability.

A desire for customer boards is the ability to reach back for further feedback; powerful connections and play-friendly relationships excel. Strategic boards are value heavy on time and high standards.

ADVICE FROM THE ADVISORS

"I think when you ask someone to be on a board, you have to say, 'I'd like you to be on my advisory board and here's why. Here's what my expectations are, and if you can live up to those expectations, I really want you. But if at any level you think you might not be able to meet those three or four or five expectations, thank you for considering,' and then move on. You are going to get people who are wholly invested."

~ Bob Gold

Following is a list of tips and tricks for your invitation package. You'll want to send it out and follow up!

INVITATION PITCH DECK

ABB Approach

Tell your story in a fast and engaging way. My clients generally put together an invitation pitch deck using the Slidedoc guidelines because it is one of the most compelling and easy to read types of documents.

A Slidedocs piece is based on the work of Nancy Durate and explored in her book *Slidedocs*. It is a mixture of narrative information from a presentation (compelling pictures) combined with key information from a text-only document. This book you are currently reading uses a variation of the Slidedoc approach, which makes it easier to read and understand examples than a document that is only text. This approach creates a very reader-friendly and impactful company introduction.

Make this piece compelling. At this time it is more about the sizzle than the steak. You want them to buy into the vision and the opportunity, so open the curtains and let them glimpse inside. Create a company timeline and highlight some of your major milestones or accomplishments. Introduce the key players at the company. At this stage you want to use these items to represent the gist of the business.

CONTRACTS AND COMPENSATION

Compensation

No doubt as you've been eagerly absorbing all that you can about advisory boards, the big question has been lurking under the surface: *How much will this cost?*

The truth is, the cost can vary immensely. Before delving into methods of figuring out the cost, you will benefit more from asking: *How much money will this make for me?*

Start answering on a personal value level by considering these questions:

1. What would it be worth to your bottom line if you had one new proven revenue source you would never have thought of?

    ▸ Hint: Think triple your revenues.

2. What would it be worth if you avoided a very costly mistake or were able to improve efficiencies exponentially?

    ▸ Hint: Think double your productivity.

3. What would it be worth if you were introduced to a new level of business you could not have easily reached on your own?

    ▸ Hint: Think quadruple your valuation.

4. What would be the monetary value of increasing your professional credibility and access to key players for you and your company.

    ▸ Hint: Priceless.

When I ask my clients those questions, the numbers range from the high six figures to seven figures without question. For example, if you had a business doing $2M and you did triple revenues what would be worth $6M? If you did double productivity what would be worth $1M? Would generating an additional $7M be worth investing 2% of these potential benefits to get these results? $7M * 0.02% = $140,000. The best part is it will not cost you anywhere near that much.

One way to look at it would be to do a cost per advisor approach. In this case, for a board of seven advisors, that's $20,000 each. If that makes you at all hesitant to go after seriously senior people, it shouldn't because you will be offering a small piece of equity with some costs.

As we explored in Part 1, the primary reason people join advisory boards is the fantastic opportunity to give back and be involved. Expenses, an honorarium, and the simple chance to offer an opinion will often suffice. You may add a vested stock option, which we will cover in this section.

What is important is to be sure you maximize the time you have with them. If they feel appreciated, and know they are having a positive impact, that may be their greatest reward. Remember, many of these people may be friends, or friends of friends. As long as you are fully committed, listening, and implementing their ideas, good things will happen.

Other factors that will impact compensation

Time requirements

These advisors will not typically be charging you an hourly rate — if they did you would probably be spending tens of thousands of dollars per hour! So be wise and honest with time in your preparation and communication.

The opportunity

If the opportunity for growth is substantial, that is exciting. If you choose to offer equity ownership to your advisors, you are increasing their vested interest in your company, which typically increases your access to them.

Vested interest encourages board members to bring more than just advice and expertise to the table. One current opportunity trend is the use of phantom stocks.

> **What is a phantom stock?**
> A phantom stock is contracted between a corporation and its recipient, wherein the stock can be converted to a cash payment at a designated time or future date. Payment is tied to a corporation's market value for its equivalent number of shares. As the stock rises and falls, the payout will increase and decrease respectively, but payment is not given during these fluctuations.

All compensation is usually a combination of fees and equity. Key factors that will contribute to the level of compensation are the company's place and time in its life cycle and the level of funds available. Although this book is targeted towards High Growth Firms (HGF) that need help from business experts and / or customers, new companies can and do receive a lot of benefits from bringing in experts to help guide the way.

Startups

Many startups form an advisory board to give them credibility through association with key players. All too often I see startups ask people to be on their advisory boards, and possibly have a mentor-type conversation with the advisor, but never capitalize on getting the group together at the same time.

Because startups typically have no money and are looking for investment, they often have to use equity as a form of compensation, both to the advisors and even the facilitator.

For startups, phantom shares can be used in lieu of stock options to provide prospective contributors with a simple form of equity participation. The phantom share grants can be tied to negotiated vesting schedules, with the payout being tied to a change of control or liquidity event such as an IPO or acquisition. Both the startup and the recipients benefit from the flexibility of the agreement and the minimal legal and tax filing paperwork involved.

Growth and Establishment / Expansion

This is typically where companies who have reached a certain plateau, or are growing so fast they "don't know what they don't know," achieve the most significant results from advisory boards. For established companies, phantom shares can be used as a cash bonus plan, although some plans pay out benefits in the form of shares.

Charity

Generally speaking there is little or no compensation for advisory board members of not-for-profits and charities. Many advisors do it to increase their sphere of influence and to give back to the community.

Often a role the advisors play is one of fund-raising. One expectation is to bring funds as well as expertise and connections. This type of advisory board is typically a working board. Its advisors are expected to work on projects outside of the key meetings.

SAMPLE LETTER OUTLINE

Invitation to Board of Advisors — [*Make this as compelling as possible*]

[Date]
[Advisor's Name]
[Advisor's Company]
[Address]
[City], [State / Province], [Zip / postal code]

Dear [First Name],

I am writing to invite you to join the board of advisors of [Company formal name here]. I feel your experience in business, as well as your knowledge of the [your industry] industry and of [Company], would be a tremendous contributor to our success.

The purpose of this letter is to set forth our understanding of the terms of your participation with [Company], including your role and compensation. It is important to us that your involvement makes a tangible, measurable, and profitable contribution. It is also important that you are inspired to support [Company] over time and to focus your energies on successfully and efficiently contributing to our company goals. Ideally, your start date would be [Starting Date].

We propose the following:

Participation / advice regarding

[Specify what you want from the advisor. Do they offer financial expertise? Product development experience?]

[Quarterly meetings to review the course and direction of [Company]].

[Planning and organizing.]

[Product development, production, marketing.]

Compensation

[If offering equity, you want to keep the offer limited to stock options. Actual shares of stock would become taxable to the advisor.]

Upon acceptance of this offer you will be granted an option to purchase [100] shares of [Company] common stock, fully vested, and otherwise under the terms and conditions of the [Company] incentive stock option plan, for [each advisory board meeting, or per month, or ...]. In addition, you will receive 1 Option for each Net Income Before Tax (NIBT) dollar earned, up to a maximum of [12,000] shares per year to a total maximum of [Thirty-six Thousand] Share

Options (36,000). In the event of an acquisition or public offering, [Company] shall pay your option exercise.

Hold Harmless

We understand that your primary concern is that you be retained only as an advisor by [Company], and that all decisions be reached as a result of the independent judgment of the executives of [Company]. Accordingly, should any action against [Company] in law, equity, or government regulation result from any action or decision made in whole or in part as a result of your advice, or during your participation on our board of advisors, [Company] shall indemnify you and hold you harmless from any claim.

Understood, Agreed, & Accepted

By signing this offer as your acceptance, and returning it by [Date], you acknowledge and agree that the terms set forth in this letter constitute our entire understanding and agreement regarding your advisorship.

_____   _____
[Owner/Founder]   [Advisor's Name]
Founder & CEO   [Advisor's Company]
[Company]

ADVICE FROM THE ADVISORS

"Start with the contract. You must have clearly set expectations. You also need to keep them emotionally engaged. Send out an email with the top five great things that are happening with your company. If you don't keep them engaged, they will drift.

A few clients have secured advisors by giving them stock up front, which I would advise against because once they have stock they have stock, and it is hard to get it back. Instead, do a two- to three-year term and vest the stock over the term. If someone wants more stock then they can become a senior advisor, and they have a greater commitment to you. Milestone-based vesting of stock is best — when you hit these key things you get more equity. That way everyone is focused on the deliverables."

~ Christine Comaford

3) PREPARATION

Lead, Prepare, and Direct the Board

ONBOARDING

Congratulations! You have reached out and secured a great set of people. You have an advisory board committed to working with you and growing your company to the next level. Your advisory board is a real thing, and this book was worth the investment!

In the onboarding process you want to ensure that all of your members are fully up to speed. It's time to open the company books and share the nuts and bolts.

> Some people use the invitation letter as a letter of intent as well. Before you embark on the full onboarding process, it is crucial that you have a signed contract, especially if equity is part of the agreement. Once the legalities are handled — which are like a game of hop scotch compared to the legalities for a board of directors — you can press on. Because there is no fiduciary liability for an advisor, there is very little risk for either party.

Now that they have signed on, get them up to speed as quickly as possible. Welcome them and give them key preliminary information about your organization.

The onboarding package of a strategic advisory board provides the following:

- Organizational chart
- Latest business plan or strategic plan
- Financials (last two years' financial statements, budgets)

It may also include (optional):

- Marketing and sales collateral
- Operations manual
- Quarterly reports
- Product roadmap
- Customer survey results

More information equals more help offered.

This is where you break the seal on the company vault! You must let these people know what you are struggling with and what your biggest challenges are. The more information you withhold, the less effective your board will be. Instead of bombarding them at your first meeting, your onboarding package provides them the time and space to deeply consider your situation.

Governance

In a not-for-profit / community advisory board, governance becomes more applicable. Governance, or the way an organization is managed, is often talked about as very important for board meetings, but again this usually refers to boards of directors, where governance is paramount. Many of the values set out in the image below are equally valuable for your advisory board.

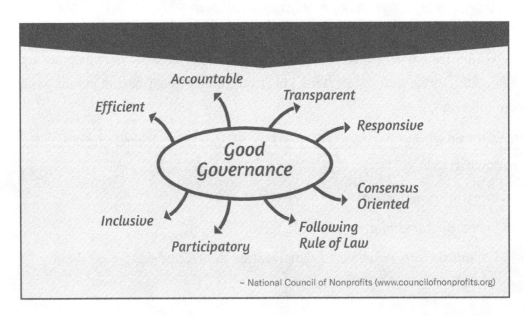

~ National Council of Nonprofits (www.councilofnonprofits.org)

ABB APPROACH

Since advisory boards should be less formal and more interactive, it is more fun to refer to governance as the *rules of play*. Again, because there is no fiduciary liability associated with being on an advisory board, governance is not as strictly followed. Having said that, when advisors know the rules of play in advance the whole game moves more smoothly. It is always helpful to spell out any rules in writing.

PREPARATION

The information presented above lays the foundation for the advisors to know and understand the company. Now we have to map out all the different meetings and communications the advisory board will need to schedule. Often, this will include in-person meetings and online meetings and any other time requirement throughout the year.

A key document is the challenge statement, which has more specific information on the challenges and topics to be addressed at the meeting. This is usually given to the advisors a couple of weeks prior to the actual meeting. The challenge statement sets up the desired outcome for that particular meeting and will give the advisors specific things to think about before the meeting.

Ongoing Communications

You need a communications plan. A lot of information and communication needs to flow to maximize the relationship. As well as onboarding material, provide some of the following as your communication continues:

- Interviews
- Surveys
- Reports
- Project Progress

> There are great software solutions in the marketplace to help with customer advisory boards. This software is often adaptable to other boards. It keeps all the parties up to date on progress and changing requirements.
>
> **Recommended:** Impetus Software is an excellent tool to make collaboration and communication run better *(https://www.impetusdigital.com)*.
>
> Designed by two Canadian women, Impetus believes in disrupting the way companies interact and seek advice from key opinion leaders and C-Suite Executives by using convenient, asynchronous online forums and digital tools.

4) PLANNING

Design Ultra Productive Board Meetings and Winning Outcomes

An amazing meeting depends on two important components: design and logistics.

The creation of an event requires attention to a lot of details. A comment by an Adobe executive that one of the most important elements for having a customer advisory board is having someone who is a great event manager reflect as much.

Planning is split into two parts: logistics and meeting design. All the event management aspects will go under logistics, while the real magic is created by the intentional planning and design of the meeting itself. This is where you can choose the best facilitation techniques and tools to make the meetings memorable and productive.

This is a very important meeting, so it is paramount that you get it right.

LOGISTICS

As your recruits are at home celebrating their new role as your advisory board members, you need to be hard at work planning logistics for your first big meeting. This is a big event in the history of your company. Make sure it goes off without a hitch.

PRE-MEETING

When the big day comes for your board to meet, it needs to be a great advisor experience. They should be so well-informed that they walk into the room for the first time with a great feeling and everyone comes in at the same level. The best way for that to happen is to take care of the specifics ahead of time. Plan it, and plan it right. Decide what to share ahead with your advisors. The clearer the picture they receive ahead of time, the more value they can deliver.

Information items to keep your team informed:

- A meeting date that works for everyone
- A calendar with key dates highlighted
- When you will contact them
- What homework they'll get
- Clear expectations about subjects you'll be dealing with
- A full meeting agenda prior to arrival

A sample event planner checklist might include:
- a good location
  — research locations and consider individual needs of the board
- catering: food and refreshments
- equipment
  — whiteboard, speakers, projector, pens, and pads
- accommodations
  — hotel options
  — preferences of members
  — special needs and considerations
- transportation
  — flights
  — ground transportation to hotel
  — transportation to meeting venue
  — local transportation for personal time, including transit fares
- city information
- day trips
- events
- a map of the city
- thank you gifts
- an after event
  — this offers relationship-building opportunities and helps the board let off steam. It also offers opportunity for fun and furthers positive associations.

It will help to conduct a quick survey ahead of time, highlighting business topics and issues. Use the replies from your board to help guide the meeting agenda. The survey should also be focused on learning about your board members so that you can cater to the specifics of the meeting itself, and also ensure their comfort while under your care.

MEETING LOGISTICS

A meeting has a lot of moving parts, and the success of the event will depend on how smoothly everything comes together. Think like an event planner, and you won't miss a beat.

ADVICE FROM THE ADVISORS

"The best way to do an advisory board meeting is to invite them to an off-site. Off-site meetings were one of the most critical components of the success of Atari and Chucky Cheese. The off-site almost needs to be an overnight. Far enough away that you do not have to rush back to get home.

It flips a switch in the brain that says, "I'm here for an outcome," and because of the remoteness and by immersing yourself in the goal / challenge you really get to focus. With an off-site, facilitation can be more impactful and ensure that, even with a soft agenda, we get the outcomes we wanted to create."

~ Nolan Bushnell

MEETING DESIGN

It is 100% necessary to hire a professional facilitator for your meeting, because as the business owner you need to be fully engaged in the discussions rather than running the meeting. A professional facilitator brings many benefits to ensure that your advisory board meeting is effective.

While your advisors might come at a reasonable rate, your facilitator probably won't. With the level of growth your board can offer and the quality of people you will work with, the facilitator expense is a necessity. Their skill in keeping the meeting on track and bringing forth myriad ideas in a well-formulated climate will optimize the advisory board outcome. In Part 3, we will go into more detail about running great meetings.

ABB APPROACH

One of the best ways to reverse engineer a meeting is to storyboard its design. Once you've designed the meeting, you can include the outline in the agenda you send your advisors ahead of time. This is another great visualization tool that will help you design an outstanding meeting.

Here is a brief guide to storyboarding your meeting on a topic-by-topic level. Simply answer each question for each of the meeting's topics:

- What is the topic?
- What is the purpose of exploring this topic?
- What exercise or facilitation technique matches this topic?
- Who will facilitate?
- How long will it take?

MEETING DESIGN – STORYBOARDING

Date and Time
Participants

TOPIC	GOAL	GAME/ Exercise	WHY	STEPS/ Timing	LEADER/ FACILITATOR

~ Liberating Structures, *https://www.liberatingstructures.com*

Begin by outlining all the key outcomes you want to achieve in your meeting. Then choose the best exercises or set-ups to achieve the desired results. This is a great time to work alongside your facilitator for these activities.

To have a really great advisory board meeting, it is critical to be sure that you are getting as much information from your advisors as possible. Listen more than you speak. Ignite Advisory Group are the leaders in customer advisory board (CAB) consulting for the technology sector. Some of their big-name clients include Adobe and Iron Mountain. One of their central messages is to be diligent about the ratio of speaking to listening when it comes to meetings. Increase your listening ratio and you'll learn more and achieve better results for the most beneficial meeting outcomes.

> A best practice to follow for your meetings is the 80/20 rule. Ignite Advisory Group outlines the three levels of CAB maturity of speaking and listening ratios.
>
> **Immature — You speak for 80% and listen for 20%**
>
> You often see this with inexperienced companies. They spend lots of money to bring their customers together and then spend most of the time wanting to impress with their PowerPoint presentation. Their finale goes something like: "What do you think?" But where's the time remaining for advisors to answer?
>
> **Competent — You speak for 50% and listen for 50%**
>
> When companies begin to have better processes in place, the meetings become more balanced with a reasonable interchange between the company and the CAB members. This is when a company has sent out some relevant information in a timely manner throughout the year with more updates between meetings.
>
> **Mature — you speak for 20% and listen for 80%**
>
> If you've given all of your relevant information up-front to your members, this can be easily accomplished with the right meeting plan and facilitator.

A trained facilitator will be able to move the group and meeting to a mature stage. They can help when they see topics creeping in that are screaming "time waster" to keep the meeting moving in a positive direction. As smart business people who have been well prepared, advisors are equipped to digest information and infer meaning. It is the meaning they want to bring to you, not the time spent digesting — receiving the information far enough in advance ensures your advisors can bring their best thoughts and leave the leftovers at home.

Proper meeting design is the most underestimated step and a very critical piece. You cannot wing it. You cannot have a boring meeting. You must be intentional in order to attain the results you want. Use fun facilitation techniques to make it interactive and engaging. Wow your advisors with productive, informative, innovative, and rewarding meetings.

5) PERFORMANCE

Implement and Update: Put ideas into action with updates that cause board members to feel heard, heeded, and trusted.

This is where the rubber hits the road. It is great to receive so much support and advice for growing your company, but you need to put those strategies into an action plan. The action plan should have some key metrics and Key Performance Indicators (KPIs) to ensure that things happen in an organized and timely manner. You want to get results, and be sure you share those results with the advisory board members. When they see the impact of their advice, you showcase their value, so it is crucial to tell them about your successes and about hitting key milestones along the way. Often this means motivating your team to make things happen and create new projects that need to be managed and drive performance initiatives.

> In his brilliant book *Drive*, Daniel Pink talks about what motivates people. This is as relevant for the team executing the projects as it is for the advisors. These motivations are purpose, mastery, and autonomy.
>
> **Purpose**: Put the work in context of what is important and how it fits into the bigger picture.
>
> **Mastery**: It is important not only to recognize the mastery of the advisors but also watch your team and see what they are interested in learning about. Then, if possible, transfer some of the learning from the advisory board meetings to those team members who would benefit from the insights and knowledge.
>
> **Autonomy**: As long as you have clearly expressed the outcomes and expectations, let your advisors and team members do it any way they want. You do not want to micromanage anyone. In fact, innovative ideas come from letting people come up with a solution on their own or in collaboration.

Here are a few ways to implement the ideas and update the board members so that they feel heard, heeded, and trusted:

1. Management communication
    - ▶ advice becomes part of the strategic planning
2. Internal communication
    - ▶ Recognition within the company
3. External communication
    - ▶ Highlights in newsletters / press release

You're in the experience of your business' opportunity of a lifetime and you are overflowing with empowerment, ideas, and strategies. You don't want to lose any of this material, nor its momentum. Communicate with your advisors. Feed the relationships that feed your development. This is where you can achieve an even greater return on your investment.

Communication points to provide your advisors:

- Follow-up report: include the meeting report and summarize insights and strategies that arose from the gathering
- List of key projects planned
- Project management plans
- Metrics to track those projects

Think of some ways to stay connected to your board. Ask yourself:

- Are there internal or external communication strategies that can be implemented now?
- How will advisors be kept connected to and informed by the company? On what basis and timeline?

- Were any ideas for communication with the company's clients created?
  - ▶ For instance, an advisor-run blog or marketing material
- Is there a PR opportunity to reflect the involvement of your board members to the public?
- Is there insider information and key milestones they should know about?
  - ▶ Treat them as a senior leadership team.
- How can we make them feel their contributions were worthwhile?
- How can we respond to their needs?
  - ▶ Include anything they wish to expand upon from the meeting — through business or connections made and desired.

Whatever the action plan they help you develop, they become part of the communications plan.

PART THREE

THE ULTIMATE MEETING BLUEPRINT

> *The majority of meetings should be discussions that lead to decisions.*
>
> ~ Patrick Lencioni

THE ART OF THE MEETING

> *"I find most meetings are a waste of time. They are so ill-prepared and there's little opportunity for true synergy in producing better solutions than what anyone originally thought of. So I work hard to only attend meetings that have strategic importance and miss all kinds of other seemingly urgent meetings."*
>
> ~ Stephen Covey

Once your advisory board is in place, it's time to plan your first meeting. This could be one of the most important meetings for the company because it will have strategic importance, and the value of the time of the people in the room is priceless. You must ensure that this meeting is not a time-waste but the most engaging, well-prepared, and results-oriented meeting possible. Planning an effective meeting is an art that works best with structural integrity.

> Meetings are an opportunity to get lots of great information, make key decisions, and find innovative solutions. You can categorize meetings into the following types:
> - **Collaborative:** plan and problem solve
> - **Presentational:** provide information
> - **Directional:** make decisions, feed information forward, or give people feedback

With any one of these three structures a meeting is a great opportunity — yet many top managers claim that 67% of meetings are unproductive. If you're used to dreading unproductive meetings, or think your attendees may be doing so, check out the infographic below to see the surprising statistic of how many billions of dollars are lost per year on meetings.

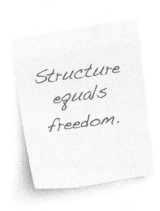

Structure equals freedom.

~ https://www.inc.com/laura-montini/infographic/the-ugly-truth-about-meetings.html

Meetings cost money. If you do them right, you can get a good return on investment (ROI). First, you need to know what that investment is. Knowing this, you may give more thought to the length of the meeting and who really needs to be there.

> The following logical formula will give you the true cost of a meeting:
> Meeting Cost = Meeting Length + Hourly Wage of Attendees

In designing your meeting, start with the end result in mind and then reverse engineer it. What is the desired outcome of the meeting? What solution do you want to come away with? If you are going to have a meeting to discuss a major decision, then a directional meeting format, focused on the desired outcome, is the way to go.

Each meeting is an investment of time and money because everyone in the room has a minimum hourly rate. You must consider all the planning details in order to maximize the value of this investment.

From the Archives

In a case where I project-managed a new software system, the initial proposal was dismissed before the committee had a chance to fully consider it.

We were exploring a new software system designed to solve a key problem. Part way into the process the enterprise architect returned a firm "No" but did not provide a reason or a solution. As the project manager, I then had to set up several more meetings with the enterprise architect, the product owner, senior back-end developer, and the head of operations. The cost was easily over $500/hour. After a one-month delay and thousands of dollars down the drain, we went ahead with the initial proposed solution — which cost less than the meetings!

> **Lesson: What happens when someone says "No" but doesn't offer an alternative solution? Ask them, "If you don't want us to do this, what *do* you want us to do?"**

If the organization had taken a step back and considered the cost of these meetings vs. testing the proposed solution they would have saved significant money and time. Because the original solution was discarded without rational discussion it never actually died. Instead, it became the "elephant in the room" that infected the other ideas that arose through a stream of costly and unproductive meetings.

Symptoms of a bad meeting

- Boring: the feeling of death by PowerPoint
- Falling asleep: after-lunch meetings are the worst, when "food comas" can hit
- Never-ending: the feeling that some people love to hear themselves speak
- Multi-tasking: smartphones have added another distraction to meetings

But meetings needn't be like this. You can come out of an effective meeting inspired, feeling that you have made a contribution, and then follow that inspiration up by taking ownership of your piece and your commitment to the team that makes it happen.

Use diligence when assembling the right meeting participants.

Any type of meeting demands the time of its participants. Because we know that time is valuable, it often feels as if meetings are, in and of themselves, all that is required. I attended, therefore I know! But a well-executed meeting will pull its attendees into a powerful consciousness, which will spark an energy and involvement that guides everyone through their follow-up tasks.

Preparation and great facilitation lay the groundwork for stability, action, and accountability. Interactive components aid in conscious mental involvement and connectivity. Games provide emotional and energetic rewards. Together, these components facilitate idea growth and forward momentum.

The biggest current trend is to make things more interactive — engage people; give everyone a voice. Have tools and techniques that work equally for the extroverts and the introverts. An example of this is "silent storming" (brainstorming on post-it notes prior to the conversation).

Probably the greatest mistake is holding a meeting that goes on too long. Habitual work trends create hour-long meetings when ten minutes are needed. Be wary of automatic calendar booking settings that over-schedule while you're looking the other way.

The daily stand-up meeting has become a key practice in the agile world, which operates on short iterative project management methodology used primarily in software development. It's a brilliant combination of physical engagement — standing up for the whole meeting — and time-boxing to 15 minutes.

> A stand-up meeting, by definition, is one where everyone stands up around a table or board and answers three key questions:
> 1. What have I done?
> 2. What am I doing next?
> 3. What is standing in my way?

Leadership coach Jason Womack over at *www.Inc.com* suggests breaking up your entire day into 96 different 15-minute blocks. This will mean that meetings can be as short as 15 minutes and no one will book one hour for a decision that could be made in 45 minutes.

15-minute stand-up meetings are becoming more popular beyond just agile and fast growing companies. Because so many meetings are disruptive and dysfunctional, a best practice for helping your teams stay productive is setting core work hours, such as from 11:00am–2:00pm when no-one is allowed to attend meetings.

Time cannot be re-gifted. Use it wisely.

Here is an example of a poster to protect your team's core hours.

This consistent measure eliminates employee griping about sacrificed work time, as it gives employees an extended block time to work without disruptions. With a set time to focus on their tasks, they can get into a flow state and be much more productive. People will still be pulled into meetings but not in a disruptive way. This forces everyone to be more strategic about their meetings. It ensures that once in the meeting everyone is focused on the task at hand. They won't be multi-tasking or thinking of the other work they need to get done.

Recent reports acknowledge that multi-tasking is not productive. MIT neuroscientist Earl Miller notes that our brains are "not wired to multitask well ... when people think they're multitasking, they're actually just switching from one task to another very rapidly. And every time they do, there's a cognitive cost."

A good meeting is like a well-choreographed dance routine. All the steps and the timing need to be done in advance and rehearsed. If people aren't prepared, or the meeting is not properly run, it becomes an invisible waste of time where no one talks in the meeting, everyone talks after the meeting.

However, when meetings do go well — when solutions are created and the information is effectively delivered — it is important to recognize these successes. Celebrate all successes, from big ones like landing a big contract to small ones like fixing a smaller problem. Recognition and celebration are fundamental in remunerating your team.

From the Archives

LITTLE things make a BIG difference.

I was working with a small cross-functional team. The back-end developer was a very senior player who had a lot of people vying for his time and expertise on other projects. He had a reputation for being gruff and distant. At the end of the first project I wanted to celebrate with the team, but the company did not allocate any money for this purpose. I created award certificates on my computer, put them in frames from the dollar store and convinced a supplier to buy pizza. We had a nice celebratory lunch.

When we moved offices, I was surprised and delighted to see the award hanging in a prominent spot in the developer's new space. I am also pleased to say that from then on he always happily gave priority to my projects!

Lesson: People really do value being appreciated.

In an advisory board setting, your advisors are often doing it for the contribution more than the money. Celebrating is a great way to recognize contribution.

Preparation

"The magic to a great meeting is all of the work that's done beforehand."

~ *Bill Russell*

The more preparation you do, the more productive you will be. People often put an agenda together to talk of issues. Most forget to reverse engineer their meetings with the outcome they want to achieve.

> **Reverse Engineer**
> For the purpose of this book, think of the desired outcome you want to achieve and then figure out each step required to get there. Don't stop until all the key steps are clear.

In a meeting where a key decision is required, think through decision-making processes that will help you get the desired results. Your purpose will be clearly understood.

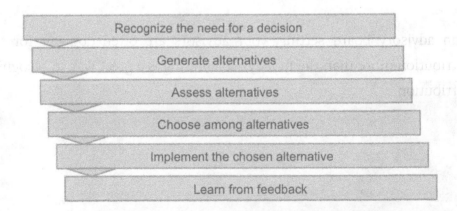

A good meeting motivates people. In Daniel Pink's book *Drive*, he talks about what motivates people in the context of a meeting. The key factors he discusses are:

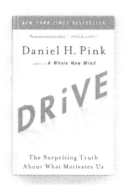

- **Purpose:** state a clear goal
- **Mastery:** make sure people have the knowledge in advance and that you bring in the right people with the right knowledge
- **Autonomy:** give them some space to do it their own way and contribute to the meeting.

A big part of preparing a great meeting is to create an environment where people are encouraged to bring up different ideas, and feel free to have great conversations where these ideas are accepted and discussed. To be productive, you need to have a working session where you roll up your sleeves and bang out the work. At the end of the meeting, have action items that people own, meaning they will self-volunteer and commit to completing them by a deadline. Keep this in mind when preparing.

A great tool for reverse engineering a meeting is a storyboard meeting designer. This was discussed in Part 2, but let's now go into more detail on how to use it.

Storyboarding is one of the many tools and techniques outlined in the ground-breaking book *The Surprising Power of Liberating Structures — Simple Rules to Unleash A Culture of Innovation*, by Henri Lipmanowicz & Keith McCandless. The authors provide a selection of tools that defy conventional structures and help organizations unleash innovation. Many of the structures in the book have worked incredibly well for my clients.

Conventional structures are either too inhibiting (presentations, status reports, and managed discussions) or too loose and disorganized (open discussions and brainstorms) to creatively engage people in shaping their own future. They frequently generate feelings of frustration and / or exclusion and fail to provide space for good ideas to emerge and germinate. This means that huge amounts of time and money are spent working the wrong way. More time and money are then spent trying to fix the unintended consequences.

*~ Liberating Structures,
https://www.liberatingstructures.com*

The Design Story Board Tool

Define Step-by-Step Elements for Bringing Meetings to Productive Endpoints

As first introduced in the Planning section of Part 2, using this tool is one of many unique approaches the ABB recommends, as it is an effective way to design meetings. It allows you to clearly layout the important outcomes you want to achieve, explore different tools to achieve those outcomes, why a particular tool is a good choice, and the timing and skills needed to make that happen. It also provides a framework for you to prototype different approaches. This will ensure your meeting design is working toward the outcome you intend. Without a planned storyboard to lead you, the flow and the exercises may not get you to where you want to go.

Below is a sample of a blank storyboard from the Liberating Structures menu. You can use it to help design your meeting's agenda. It will ensure the outcomes desired.

MEETING DESIGN – STORYBOARDING

Date and Time
Participants

TOPIC	GOAL	GAME/ Exercise	WHY	STEPS/ Timing	LEADER/ FACILITATOR

~ Liberating Structures, *https://www.liberatingstructures.com*

An agenda with no context is not very powerful. Typically an agenda looks like this:

- one sentence about the meeting objective
- a list of topics
- a list of who will be attending

The Visual Communications section unfolds some of these minute-taking tools further.

To maximize effectiveness, put the time in ahead, rather than allowing the meeting to dictate the information. Respect and set your prep time to take your understanding and efforts further before stepping into the meeting room. Be intentional about the design of the meeting so that you can make it more participative and interactive. To make an agenda better and ensure more productivity, build the following into your meeting plan:

- **Create a storyboard:** use as a planning tool and then translate it into a more comprehensive agenda that says what you are doing and why.
- **Scrutinize your attendee list with purpose:** when selecting participants, remember that meetings cost money, and that includes time taken from pertinent players by voices that aren't needed on a particular topic.
- **Plan ahead to reflect later:** consider how you will record the meeting. Standard pen and paper minutes take someone out of their role — whether it be the assistant you call to sit in and record or a meeting member sacrificing their space to take notes. Visual, audio recordings that can be turned into one-page summaries, Slidedocs, or meeting summary decks will stimulate the memory in post-meeting reflections and increase follow-up results. It's like having an instant replay when you need it!

A Meeting Checklist

What to bring to the meeting and how to prepare the room, including how this will be done.

- **Snacks:** All good meetings have snacks, so curate a menu that satisfies the atmosphere. Cookies are cheap and make people smile if it's small scale. Veggies keep folks alert and sandwiches satisfy for a longer duration. Coffee, tea, water, and presto — your snacks are complete!
- **Manage by the clock:** avoid conversation traps and rabbit holes by having effective time-keeping techniques such as a clock on the screen.
- **Ban technology:** This growing trend is returning people in meetings everywhere to a blissful state of focus! So, while you're at it, you should avoid distractions and multitasking — even if you believe you're a wiz, it sets a poor example.
- **Plan parking and share the information:** for anyone arriving from off-site, this saves a big headache and starts your meeting off right. Reaching out in this way to eliminate exterior annoyances demonstrates thoughtfulness and respect.
- **Energy management preparation:** keep the meeting flow and balance by considering your own energy and that of others ahead of time. Use tools that allow people to move around to adjust the room to its most effective state.

Preparing for a meeting when you are presenting requires a different kind of preparation. You need to prepare the presentation, practice, and feel confident. Use the following ideas to prepare yourself to present in a meeting.

Presentations

Start by putting ideas on index cards. These are stories on idea cards so you can shuffle the deck to perfect the flow. What goes in the beginning, the middle, and the end? Insert the stories where they can add impact. Each key point has an index card so you can move it around. Then test out the presentation and make adjustments.

From the Archives

The good: *The most well-received presentation I ever gave was at the Project Management Institute (PMI), Marketing Services Community. What made this experience effective was that we did four dry runs with the organizers. Since they all came from a marketing background, the input was amazing. Each iteration got better and better. My final presentation did not resemble the presentation I started with!*

The bad: *Presentation skills can deteriorate if they aren't used. For many years I taught an advanced motorcycle summer training course. When I began teaching, the eight-month absence really showed between seasons. I wanted a consistent quality of presentation, so I implemented a new strategy. Each cold winter month, even when riding practice was out, presentation practice became my norm. When summer arrived, I did not miss a single swerve of my speech, and it was clearly effective and settling for each class of new learners.*

Other tips to help smooth out your presentation include:

- a good night's rest;
- a protein-rich breakfast;
- an activity that creates a positive frame of mind;
- visualization and / or power poses;
- watching Ann Cuddy's TED Talk on body language;
- pre-set expectations of the presentation using a visual clock: from "here" to "here" we're dealing with this, and "here" to "here," dealing with this; and
- ensuring you have all the tools ready for exercises you may be doing — we'll get into that more in the upcoming sections.

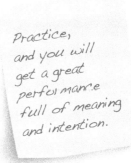

Practice, and you will get a great performance full of meaning and intention.

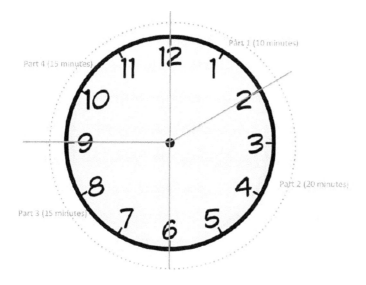

Facilitation

"We cannot teach people anything; we can only help them discover it within themselves."

~ *Galileo Galilei*

The key to optimizing any important meeting is to have a professional facilitator. If you've assembled a large group of high-value participants, having a professional facilitator will keep them engaged, keep the meeting on track, and capture the key ideas. A good facilitator will have tools and techniques to help increase participation and make it more interactive, as well as keeping things focused and getting more done faster.

These tools and techniques will lead to

- dynamic discussions;
- courageous conversations;
- interactive engagement;
- collaborative insights;
- innovative exercises;
- developing meaningful goals;
- consensus building;
- divergent thinking (coming up with lots of ideas);
- convergent thinking (prioritizing based on objectives); and
- creative problem solving.

Here are a few ways a professional facilitator can help make your meeting effective:

- **Co-create with the group or team.** When you get two or more people together solving a problem you come up with new ideas that you would never have come up with on your own or with one other person. We spoke about this earlier in "the Power of the Collective Mind."

- **Optimize a think tank.** This is a group of people who think of new ideas on a particular subject or give advice about what could be done.
- **Help with group dynamics and group dysfunctions so that you aren't left alone with all the energy management.** Facilitators care for their own emotions by staying neutral, sometimes leaving the room to steer the think tank's collective conscious. Some of a facilitator's best qualities include leading the process with tools that are based in cognitive science, and collaborative exercises that ensure that there is maximum participation.
- **Have all sorts of tools and techniques to get the outcome you want.** They will work with you to create that agenda or meeting storyboard we talked about before and will offer all sorts of innovative ideas to get you results.

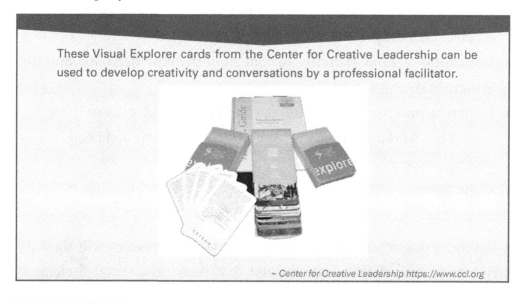

These Visual Explorer cards from the Center for Creative Leadership can be used to develop creativity and conversations by a professional facilitator.

~ Center for Creative Leadership https://www.ccl.org

Training from the Back of the Room

Another way to look at facilitation is as "training from the back of the room," based on the work of accelerated learning and training expert Sharon Bowman. Bowman's methods increase participation and movement in a meeting context (as opposed to in the classroom). Here are a few key pointers:

- movement trumps sitting
- talking trumps listening
- images trump words
- writing trumps reading
- shorter trumps longer
- different trumps same

As with the preparation stage, the idea of "beginning with the end in mind" is helpful. As you design the meeting, you can integrate some of the training ideas Bowman calls the C4s. Here is the Power Play version with a focus on facilitation.

1. **Connect** — Arrive with a good "ice breaker" so that the group can connect on a deeper level, which helps build trust.
2. **Concepts** — Frame exercises in context of the intended outcomes to achieve and set ground rules.
3. **Concrete practice** — Play "full out" and don't hold ideas or thoughts back. Keep working on the problem in a concrete way and keep digging deeper.
4. **Conclusions** — Summarize the options and review how they meet the objectives.

A facilitator doesn't dictate the perspective — your meeting will allow its members to own the discussion point, but their observational element maintains a healthy air of understanding for everyone. Often when you do an exercise, it's the debrief that is important. A good facilitator will be able to debrief an exercise, roll it up, and have people see the key solutions or lessons along the way.

An exercise could be experiential, where you solve a problem in an immersive / experiential environment. In these instances, it is the debriefing process that creates the key insights.

Clinton Swaine of Frontier Trainings has developed many courses, including a signature course on the art of being a great facilitator. He is the world leader in experiential education, and he runs a lot of games / exercises (more covered in Part 3's Gamification section). He feels this type of interaction is powerful because, "When you play a role in a simulated game it is not that it builds character, but rather it exposes character ... how did you play?" In his experiential course "Ferocious Facilitation," he clearly identifies that the facilitation roles are very different from those of a "trainer / speaker" and therefore need different skill sets. To help his students become better facilitators, he identified ten archetypes of a facilitator and the roles they need to play at any given time.

Swaine's Ten Facilitator Archetypes

~ https://frontiertrainings.com

The Philosopher

The philosopher shows up as a question. Opening possibilities, putting out alternatives, and questioning each underlying premise that appears on solid ground.

▶ The art of asking the questions

The Detective

The detective shows up with a probing mind and an inquisitive nature. Their goal is to uncover the facts and to reach the truth.

▶ The art of determining what is important

The Big Game Hunter

The big game hunter comes from a place of quiet confidence. He is humble while on the hunt, very focused and aware.

▶ The art of getting down to the real issue (white elephant hunting)

The Healer

The healer comes from a place of love, connection, compassion, and empathy. They are non-judgmental and are solely focused on the well-being of others.

▶ The art of empathy and wanting the best

The Cheerleader

The cheerleader comes from a place of connection and inspiration. They are all about elevating performance, celebrating successes, and encouraging when things look bleak.

▶ The art of inspiring winning outcomes

The Intuitive

The intuitive comes from a place of peace and tranquility. They are exceptional at staying calm under immense pressure and do not get easily flustered when challenges arise.

▶ The art of listening deeply and tapping into gut responses

The Old Time Sports Coach

The old time coach is focused on getting results. They have no problem calling out underperforming members and demanding more.

▶ The art of results and accountability.

The Storyteller

The storyteller has a unique ability to transcend culture, religion, and background and relate to people from all walks of life. The storyteller is able to use these to bypass walls, blocks, and objections and remove barriers, thus allowing learning to happen at a deep level.

> *Akin to a facilitator is someone who might call themselves a meeting coach. They are dedicated to bringing performance to its highest potential.*

▶ The art of communication and context

The Director

The director is all about resource management — the director's purpose is to help you stay calm under pressure, communicate your vision with expert precision, become accustomed to managing large groups and pull together a seamless presentation.

▶ The art of planning and keeping on schedule

The Scrambler

The scrambler uses imagery, sounds, and colors to create contrast making outrageous (even outlandish) comparisons to train the mind to be more conscious and aware.

▶ The art of creative problem solving and innovation

Whether they know it or not, the best facilitators can tap into these archetypes. They can keep people on track and improvise to get the desired outcomes.

When creating a team, understand the strengths and behavioral tendencies of your members to make the most of them. Knowing the team's behavioral traits means you can deal with unexpected comments and reactions more easily. This is the type of information a good facilitator might work with, and it helps you too.

Most people are familiar with the more traditional personality tests like Myers-Briggs and DISC. There are numerous others that provide key information to tell you where you fit.

Some helpful assessment tools for better facilitation follow.

StrengthsFinders

To help people uncover their talents

~ http://www.strengthsfinder.com/home.aspx

Kolbe

Kolbe personality test or job fit assessment test uncovers your strongest points to focus on and improve all spheres of life.

~ http://kolbe.com

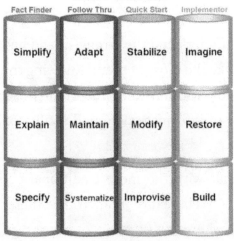

FourSight

Dedicated to the science of good thinking and problem solving, it supports the people side of innovation.

~ https://foursightonline.com

Fascination Assessment

The newer Fascination personality test by Sally Hogshead is different in that the focus comes from the other direction. As per its tagline, the test reveals "how the world sees you;" how you are fascinating. This is also the name of Hogshead's book delving into her expertise. It is based on ten years of research and helps discover the two highest values that measure how others perceive you at your best. In this assessment, Sally has identified seven core methods of communication.

7 WAYS TO ADD VALUE IN A MEETING	
POWER	HAVE A CLEAR POINT OF VIEW
INNOVATION	CREATIVELY ENGAGE, SUCH AS HUMOR
PASSION	MAKE A PERSONAL CONNECTION BEFORE AND AFTER
PRESTIGE	SET AMBITIOUS GOALS
TRUST	FOLLOW ESTABLISHED FORMAT
MYSTIQUE	ASK INTELLIGENT QUESTIONS
ALERT	SET AGENDA AHEAD OF TIME

~ https://www.howtofascinate.com

From the test, you discover your top two values, creating a matrix of 49 personality archetypes.

	INNOVATION You change the game with creativity	PASSION You connect with emotion	POWER You lead with command	PRESTIGE You earn respect with higher standards	TRUST You build loyalty with consistency	MYSTIQUE You communicate with substance	ALERT You prevent problems with care
INNOVATION You change the game with creativity	THE ANARCHY Volatile • Startling Chaotic	THE ROCKSTAR Bold • Artistic Unorthodox	THE MAVERICK LEADER Pioneering • Irreverent Entrepreneurial	THE TRENDSETTER Cutting Edge • Elite Progressive	THE ARTISAN Deliberate • Thoughtful Flexible	THE PROVOCATEUR Clever • Adept Contemporary	THE QUICK-START Prolific • Thorough Diligent
PASSION You connect with emotion	THE CATALYST Out-of-the-Box • Social Energizing	THE DRAMA Theatrical • Emotive Sensitive	THE PEOPLE'S CHAMPION Dynamic • Inclusive Engaging	THE TALENT Expressive • Stylish Emotionally Intelligent	THE BELOVED Nurturing • Loyal Sincere	THE INTRIGUE Discerning • Perceptive Considerate	THE ORCHESTRATOR Attentive • Dedicated Efficient
POWER You lead with command	THE CHANGE AGENT Inventive • Untraditional Self-Propelled	THE RINGLEADER Motivating • Spirited Compelling	THE AGGRESSOR Dominant • Overbearing Dogmatic	THE MAESTRO Ambitious • Focused Confident	THE GUARDIAN Prominent • Genuine Sure-Footed	THE MASTERMIND Methodical • Intense Self-Reliant	THE DEFENDER Proactive • Cautionary Strong-Willed
PRESTIGE You earn respect with higher standards	THE AVANT-GARDE Original • Enterprising Forward-Thinking	THE CONNOISSEUR Insightful • Distinguished In-the-Know	THE VICTOR Respected • Competitive Results-Oriented	THE IMPERIAL Arrogant • Cold Superior	THE BLUE CHIP Classic • Established Best-In-Class	THE ARCHITECT Skillful • Restrained Polished	THE SCHOLAR Intellectual • Disciplined Systematic
TRUST You build loyalty with consistency	THE EVOLUTIONARY Curious • Adaptable Open-Minded	THE AUTHENTIC Approachable • Dependable Trustworthy	THE GRAVITAS Dignified • Stable Hardworking	THE DIPLOMAT Levelheaded • Subtle Capable	THE OLD GUARD Predictable • Safe Unmovable	THE ANCHOR Protective • Purposeful Analytical	THE GOOD CITIZEN Principled • Prepared Conscientious
MYSTIQUE You communicate with substance	THE SECRET WEAPON Nimble • Unassuming Independent	THE SUBTLE TOUCH Tactful • Self-Sufficient Mindful	THE VEILED STRENGTH Realistic • Intentional To-the-Point	THE ROYAL GUARD Elegant • Astute Discreet	THE WISE OWL Observant • Assured Unruffled	THE DEADBOLT Unemotional • Introverted Concentrated	THE ARCHER On-Target • Reasoned Pragmatic
ALERT You prevent problems with care	THE COMPOSER Strategic • Fine-Tuned Judicious	THE COORDINATOR Constructive • Organized Practical	THE ACE Decisive • Tireless Forthright	THE EDITOR IN-CHIEF Productive • Skilled Detailed	THE MEDIATOR Steadfast • Composed Structured	THE DETECTIVE Clear-Cut • Accurate Meticulous	THE CONTROL FREAK Compulsive • Driven Exacting

~ https://www.howtofascinate.com

"No two personality archetypes persuade and captivate in exactly the same way."

~How the World Sees You: Discover Your Highest Value Through the Science of Fascination, by Sally Hogshead, Harper Business, 2016.

From the Archives

I've done a lot of personality assessments, as I believe in what I do and practice all the lessons I preach. I am the catalyst. My two highest values are passion and innovation. As a facilitator I add value by starting action and encouraging people to prototype their ideas to find innovative solutions.

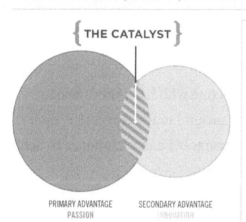

THE CATALYST
OUT-OF-THE-BOX | SOCIAL | ENERGIZING | ENTHUSIASTIC | CREATIVE

HOW THE WORLD SEES YOU

- You make a vibrant first impression and you're valued for your enthusiastic approach and ability to generate ideas
- Buoyant and social, you embrace new situations and relationships with zeal
- You speak with flair and you use expressive gestures
- You know how to captivate an audience. You're named "The Catalyst" because you add value by starting action

PRIMARY ADVANTAGE
PASSION

SECONDARY ADVANTAGE
INNOVATION

~ https://www.howtofascinate.com

As mentioned earlier, there are four distinct types of advisory boards: strategic, customer, community, and peer. The type of facilitator that suits your meeting best will be based largely on the board type and what characteristics, skills, and personality traits a particular facilitator holds and can pull out in others.

Perhaps you've done some of these personality tests and recognize your abilities in an archetype or two. Is this leading you to believe you can spare a meeting expense by acting as its facilitator? You must absolutely not act as your own facilitator. You don't have the skills, even if this book makes it seem like you do.

For real success, you need to be 100% invested in the process and ideas coming at you fast and furiously. Good business owners tend not to run great meetings for a variety of reasons. People underneath them won't speak up because, duh, their boss is in the room! Bosses aren't accustomed to being the junior person in a room full of highly successful people, and they don't have the skills to maximize and make sure they are listening 80% of the time. They don't know how to extract the most pertinent information from a room full of world-class advisors who are there to help solve the biggest challenges for the company. Sometimes, the business owner wants to justify the position rather than learn a humbling lesson.

The type of board you've assembled will help you determine what kind of facilitator to look for.

- Strategic advisory boards need someone who has experience in developing strategic conversations around marketing, sales, operations, finance, and HR. They will tend to use tools and techniques to achieve those types of conversations.

- CAB (customer advisory boards) need someone who has done some focus group work and can ask questions to uncover customer needs, pains, and gains and help validate key assumptions.

- Community advisory boards need someone who can get members to volunteer for key tasks, design a process with built-in accountability, and help develop teamwork and inspiration.

- Peer advisory boards need someone who can provide or source relevant content for the members, then manage time and contribution, as well as creating systems for accountability.

Visual Communication

Visual Thinking

"Visual thinking is the foundation for being creative and solving some of the most complex problems."

~ Lisa Kay Solomon, Founder of Innovation Studio

Artists have tools they use to create their art. They don't leave the ideas inside their heads and call it a progressive day at the easel. By getting things out of people's heads and onto the walls, meeting participants can have a shared understanding to make things more productive. In meetings, the ability to visualize information is priceless. Just watch as your board members understand the complexities of your business when presented in a visual way.

Visual communication has a wide range of benefits for ideation and communication, policy analysis, policy development, meetings, collaborative work groups, decision-making, and strategic planning. These benefits highlight the significance of this trend — visualization tools will become a key component of the most productive advisory board meetings possible.

There are a variety of trends and tools like canvases, sticky notes, mapping out ideas on the wall and mind-mapping (which most people are familiar with). These tools are fundamentally changing the way people communicate. Especially if there is a language barrier, pictures are universal and help eliminate misunderstandings.

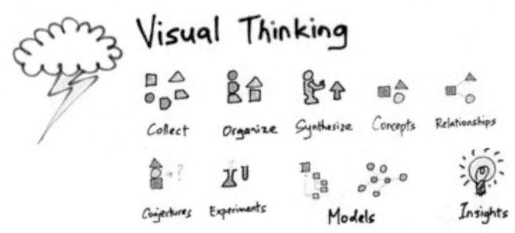

~ Visual Thinking Lab

Visual thinking is the use and exploration of images as tools for communication, understanding, analysis, and problem solving. Common visual tools include mapping tools, flow charts, timelines, and graphic recording, to name a few. There are as many thinking tools as there are people who use them. Visual thinking puts discussions on display so that everyone has a shared understanding and a shared language.

Sometimes referred to as "picture thinking" or "right-brained learning," the visual thinking method is used to easily communicate complex concepts and ideas in a short amount of time. The use of strictly verbal cues in meetings can lead to many interpretations and different understandings, but visual thinking allows people to organize thoughts in a non-verbal way.

Here we are going to explore this group of meeting tools and how to use them in your meetings.

STICKY NOTES (Post-its™)

If you walk through many Tech companies and Startups, you will often see sticky notes everywhere. These are typically "Scrum tasks boards" a highly visual tool used in Agile project management. By having all pending work displayed visually, there is

Easy-move sticky notes are an ideal tool. Questions turn into answers, information shifts, and ideas take actionable placements.

Story	To Do	In Progress	Done
Story A		Task	Task
Story B	Task	Task	Task
Story C		Task	Task

increased transparency. These boards are usually used in conjunction with the stand-up meetings discussed earlier.

Using visual task boards as a main form of communication is a gift from the Agile world of project management. This tool is a dynamic way to delegate tasks to a team. It also allows work to be quickly re-prioritized and tasks moved across the board so that progress can be tracked. In this way, it becomes obvious what work needs to be done and is being done.

In his book *Visual Meetings,* David Sibbet shows how using graphics, sticky notes, and idea mapping can transform group productivity.

Ground rules to a good sticky:
- one word or one key thought per sticky
- an image is more powerful than a word
- no bullet points — the points cannot split up if you need to re-arrange
- use a marker to allow reading from a distance
- use bold, block letters — large print

SILENT STORMING

Silent Storming is a quieter, productive way of brainstorming. Allow everyone in the room some time to think about possible solutions. Write each thought on a sticky and then put all of them up on a wall. Collectively cluster the different areas of thought, name them, and then begin a conversation.

Silent storming sets a comfortable tone for all sorts of personality types from the loudest extravert to the quietest introvert.

Everyone will have had sufficient time to reflect and contribute. With the reduced pressure to vocalize on the spot, introverts will find contribution easier. The board member innovation is increased with this versatile approach to personality types.

CANVASES

Sticky notes are also used with another amazing tool that helps create better conversations. In 2009 The Business Model Canvas was introduced by Alexander Osterwalder and Yves Pigneur, and now there are many different types of canvases.

Imagine a giant, blank chart where you can figuratively paint your business ideas. What makes it fun is that it allows you to begin to prototype your idea and explore what happens when you look at alternative models and add in different constraints. The business model canvas is one of the core canvases that started the movement, but there are many out there. The best thing about a canvas is the focused conversations you have when "painting."

In 2015, Alexander and his partners released *Value Proposition Design*, the definitive book on their value proposition canvas. This allows you to look at each customer segment separately and validate that your products and services fit with the customer's needs, pains, and gains. To download your copy go to https://strategyzer.com/canvas.

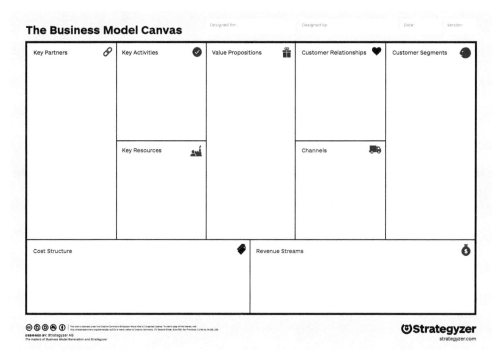

~ Osterwalder, A and Pigneur Y, Business Model Canvas

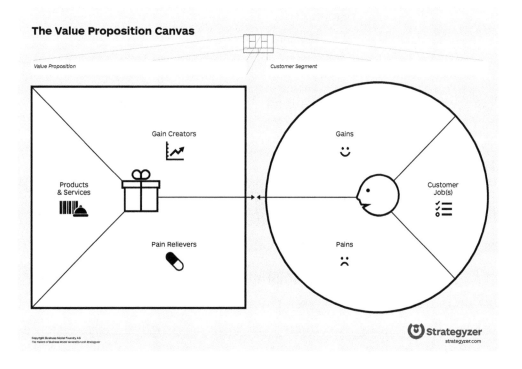

~ Osterwalder, A and Pigneur Y, Value Proposition Canvas

From the Archives

On my way to a big conference in Silicon Valley, my coach at the time told me to "get ready for something BIG." When I was first introduced to the business model canvas by creator Alexander Osterwalder, I knew this was BIG! It was the most exciting strategic planning tool I had seen in a long time. It was simultaneously engaging and interactive and captured the nine key elements that must be addressed to evaluate any product or business.

1. *Customer Segment*
2. *Value Proposition*
3. *Customer Relationship (cost of acquisition)*
4. *Channels (marketing and delivery)*
5. *Key Resources (required to deliver)*
6. *Key Activities*
7. *Key Partnerships*
8. *Cost Summary*
9. *Revenue summary*

MAPPING

There are several types of mapping. And, good news! Stickies can also be used as part of this tool.

Mind Mapping

Most people are familiar with mind mapping, which was made popular by British author and television personality Tony Buzan in 1974. It links associations and is credited with creating engaged learning.

It is a great way to get a visual imprint of a situation, and the cool thing is that your brain more readily remembers pictures. By making sure that all the ideas that come up in a meeting are captured visually, it helps make sure there is a shared understanding.

The five characteristics of mind mapping:

- The main idea, subject, or focus is plotted in the center.
- The main themes branch out from the center in any direction.
- The branches comprise an image or word drawn or printed on its associated line.
- Topics of lesser importance branch out as smaller branches of the associated theme.
- The branches form a connected nodal structure.

The following is a mind map on Tennis

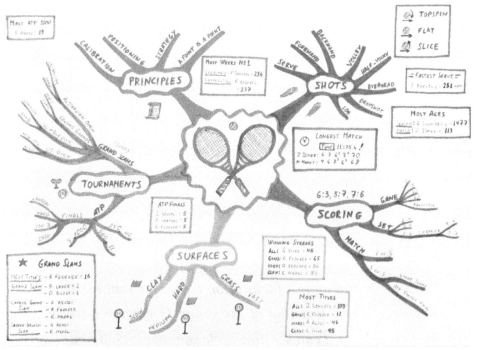

~ Tony Buzan

Dialogue Mapping

Mapping is a chameleon-like tool with a few incarnations. In his book of the same name, Jeffery Conklin explores dialogue mapping, which provides a different framework to visually capture key decision-making meetings. The mapping only goes in one direction and follows the conversation and decisions. It has some unique benefits.

The following is an example of a dialogue map.

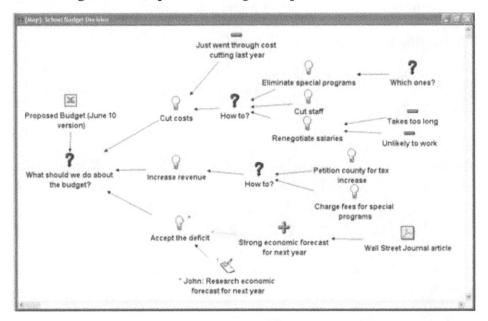

~ Jeffery Conklin

> *Dialogue mapping is a facilitation technique that allows the intelligence and learning of the group to emerge naturally. Each participant can see how their comments contribute (or don't) to the coherence and order of the group's thinking.*
>
> *~ CogNexus Institute (CogNexus.org)*

Personal Maps

This idea is from Jurgen Appello, the thought leader behind the Management 3.0 movement which looks at Agile from the management perspective. The idea is that you use a specific mind mapping exercise to get to know people. Everyone can create their own and use it as a way to introduce themselves. It can also be used to compile information on a team member on an ongoing basis — adding new pieces of information as you learn more about that person. It then becomes a quick summary to review when meeting with that person.

~ Jurgen Appello

From the Archives

Personally, I like to combine new ideas with old ideas, so I have created a mash-up of the personal map with trigger questions from the classic MacKay's 66. MacKay's 66 involves 66 facts you should know about your customer, created for the MacKay envelope company and then made popular by best-selling author Harvey Mackay.

~ http://www.harveymackay.com/wp-content/uploads/2016/01/mackay66.pdf

VISUAL DOCUMENTATION

Reporting on meetings and outcomes is a vital part of making meetings great. Nancy Durate is the champion and creator of Slidedoc Earlier in the book, I recommended doing your "invitation Pitch Deck" for your advisors because it is so effective. For the purposes of reporting, Nancy Durate's Slidedocs encourage using Powerpoint to combine the narrative images with the text used in long reports. The combination is an easy to read and visually interesting report structure that makes meeting summaries a pleasure.

~ Download the Slidedocs book at http://www.duarte.com/slidedocs/.

VISUAL INSPIRATION

Hugh McLeod of *Gapingvoidart.com* inspires companies to be more productive through the artwork on the walls. He creates culture through visual stimulus. Gapingvoid has created custom art for some of the most influential companies in the world, including Intel, AT&T, Microsoft, Roche, Zappos, and eBay and hangs in over 5,000 companies around the world. Make sure you sign up for the daily art / blog posts. Hugh and his team are changing businesses with art. Here are a few of my favorites.

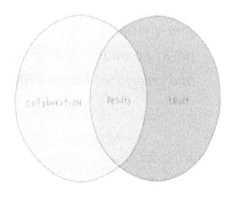

~ Hugh McLeod, https://www.gapingvoidart.com

DASHBOARDS

Visuals clarify ideas. When visuals are used to explain concepts, readers connect better. A visual brief is more effective than a text brief because if people can see what you're saying, they will understand you more clearly.

Dashboards come under the heading of Data Visualization. It is another area where you can make information more easily understood by putting it in a picture form.

> *Data visualization is a general term that describes any effort to help people understand the significance of data by placing it in a visual context. Patterns, trends, and correlations that might go undetected in text-based data but can be exposed and recognized easier with data visualization software.*
>
> *~ https://whatis.techtarget.com/*

Visualizing information also shows you have command over the subject matter and that you care enough about it to make it easily understood.

Dashboards are a great way of putting key data into a visual form so that it is easy to view and understand. Business dashboards will tend to use graphs, charts, color coding, and other images to display key metrics that a company needs to watch.

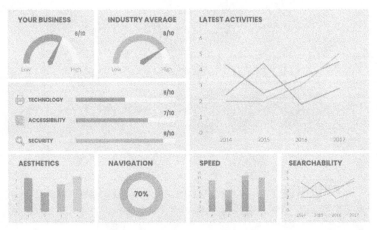

~ http://www.infographia.com/

Ideation and Innovation

Design Thinking

> *"Design Thinking is an approach to problem solving in which inspiration, ideation, and implementation occur not in sequence but as a 'system of overlapping spaces.'"*
>
> ~ Tim Brown, IDEO

Design Thinking is the driving school of thought for innovation. It encourages people to look at alternative solutions and then validate any assumptions with respect to those solutions before moving forward.

A dangerous problem in many meetings is that people can fall in love with the first solution. The company then applies time, money, and resources to execute this idea, only to have it fail. This is where design thinking comes into play. It is important to look at alternatives and then validate key assumptions with the customer or key stakeholders before making significant investments.

For the purpose of this introduction to design thinking, I'm going to touch upon only the ideas and processes used to create and define the problems / opportunities and the possible solutions for use in advisory board meetings. When you have great talent together in a room for a short period, it may be important to use some design thinking techniques to get the most value out of the time you have with them. One of the things you want to achieve in meetings is to be sure you are innovating, as this becomes the key to growth, and even to sustaining your current business.

So many companies are talking about being "customer-centric," yet very few are actually talking to their customers! To this end, the concept of design thinking is a human-centered, prototype-driven process for innovation that can be applied to products, services, and business design (processes and strategies). It always starts with looking at the problem from the customer's perspective and truly understanding the problem before even coming up with any solutions. Then you can make sure that the solution does solve the problem.

Great meetings are not just about coming up with great ideas and finding a solution to a problem. They are about having a structure to think about prototyping the business ideas and then testing to make sure your assumptions are valid.

Design thinking has many steps. The first is identifying and defining the opportunities. Next is coming up with many ideas to solve the problem and making them testable with prototypes. Finally, testing or validating the ideas to see which one is the best on different levels.

> **Inspiration:** the problem or opportunity that motivates the search for solutions.
>
> **Ideation:** the process of generating, developing, and testing ideas.
>
> **Implementation:** the path that leads from the project stage into people's lives.

~ https://www.ideo.com

IDEATION — Coming up with ideas

Design thinking processes are used in the innovation space to help people think outside the box. Ideas are often mashed up with completely different situations to see what emerges. Design thinking is about considering other possibilities before you spend time and money making something happen. Its process can be summed up in the following diagram by IDEO.

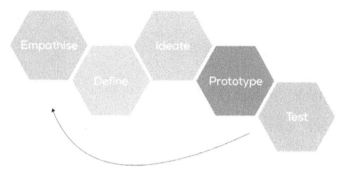

Empathize: First understand the problem or opportunity.
Define: Articulate the problem or opportunity.
Ideate: Generate unlimited possibilities.
Prototype: Create the first version of the possible best solution.
Test: Validate the solution with the customer.

~ https://www.ideo.com

VALIDATION — Testing Ideas

The Business Model Canvas can be used for prototyping business ideas.

> *First, you need to think like a surgeon. Make sure that you have the best and sharpest tools for the job. Technology has also brought some new tools to the table.*
>
> *Then you need to think like an architect. Know that your building will not be exactly like your first prototype. Look at the project from a variety of perspectives.*
>
> *Finally, you need to think like a scientist. Make sure you experiment with and test your hypothesis. Measure and test one key hypothesis at a time.*
>
> *~Alexander Osterwalder*

Validation is about going out and testing ideas and assumptions before you make a final decision, and especially before you embark on a big project.

Primary Validation techniques include:

- Interviews
- Surveys
- Focus Groups
- Prototypes
- Minimum Viable Product (MVP)
- Landing Pages

INNOVATION — Implementing Ideas

The renowned innovation company IDEO has a process of three different spaces to keep in mind when you are looking for innovative ideas.

Creativity is also a key part of innovation. The creative problem solving model is another process that is effective for innovation and brainstorming in a meeting. Creative problem solving is not your conventional approach to problem-solving. It allows people who are not trained as designers to use different creative tools to work on different challenges.

Founded in 1954, the Creative Education Foundation (CEF) is the recognized world leader in applied imagination. Alex Osborn, an ad man and educator, also invented brainstorming and co-founded the ad firm, BBDO. His classic book, *Applied Imagination*, continues to inspire.

With Sidney Parnes, Osborn developed the Osborn-Parnes Creative Problem Solving Process. For 60 years, CEF has been teaching adults and children how to use this proven process to develop new ideas, solve complex problems, and implement innovative solutions.

Every step along the way is built on a series of:

▸ divergent thinking — generating lots of ideas; and
▸ convergent thinking — using key criteria to select the most relevant ideas.

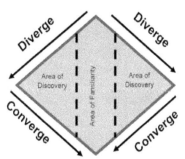

What makes this particular process so insightful is that you go through a three-step process to determine you are solving the right problem before you spend time on finding the right solution.

CLARIFY

Explore the Vision	Indentify the goal, wish, or challenge.
Gather Data	Describe and generate data to enable a clear understanding of the challenge.
Formulate Challenges	Sharpen awareness of the challenge and create challenge question that invite solutions.

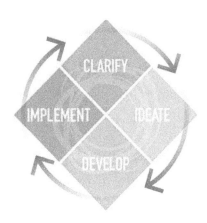

~ Creative Problem Solving Institute

Gamification

"Gamification is the process of using game thinking and game dynamics in a non-game context in order to engage audiences and solve problems."

~ Gabe Zicherman, G2 / Dopeamine

Growing research demonstrates that when people are having fun, they are more engaged. Serious games are reinventing business. A serious game is one we play to solve a business problem as opposed to other games typically played for entertainment.

According to Luke Hohmann of Conteneo, "The reason serious games are becoming so popular is because we're learning that when people are playing games, their brain is literally in a different state." Incorporating game design and game dynamics into a meeting yields better engagement and results.

> **Game thinking**: creating a customer journey by using game-like approaches to help solve problems.
>
> **Game dynamics**: crafting the experience of how a player behaves and the game interacts with the player.

"Games are the new normal."

~ Al Gore

The reason kids learn so much when they play is that playing helps build the problem-solving muscle in the brain. When applying gamification to business and meetings, it is important to understand a few things. This section includes definitions of different game types and how they can be used to get the desired meeting results.

Another leader in the gamification world is Jane McGonigal, who is currently the Director of Game Research and Development at the Institute for the Future. In her amazing life story, she built a game to help her recover from major brain trauma, not just to get better but to get super better. To date, the SuperBetter game has helped nearly half a million players tackle real-life health challenges like depression, anxiety, chronic pain, and traumatic brain injury.

In Jane McGonical's new book SUPERBETTER, she discusses how to lead a more gameful life.

> *Being gameful means bringing the psychological strengths you naturally display when you play games — such as optimism, creativity, courage, and determination — to real life. It means having the curiosity and openness to play with different strategies to determine what works best. It means building up resilience to tackle tougher and tougher challenges with greater and greater success.*
>
> *~ SuperBetter, by Jane McGonigal*

It is hard to talk about using game design to build products and businesses without looking at the work of Amy Jo Kim. Her work is focused on game dynamics and how to build out the fastest and most effective Minimal Viable Product (MVP) using both a canvas and structuring the player's (customer) journey.

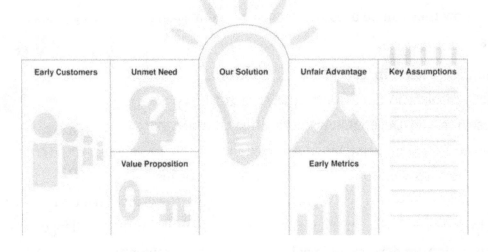

~ Amy Jo Kim, https://gamethinking.io

Introducing gamification does not mean you have to be a video gamer. It means taking the lessons of what makes games so engaging and fun and integrating them into your business so that you and your team can work more "gamefully." The common element in all types of games can be summed up as follows: a clear goal.

Business games can be categorized by three types:

1. Achievement / Behavioral Modification
2. Social / Collaborative
3. Immersive / Simulations

Players can be categorized by four types:

- Create
- Compete
- Collaborate
- Explore

1) Behavioural Modification

The idea here is that you incentivize and modify behavior using the following pathway:

> Challenge — Achievement — Reward

Every time you achieve something, the reward is associated with the release of dopamine in your brain. Dopamine is often referred to as a "wonder drug" because it makes you feel wonderful. Interestingly, people can get a dopamine buzz from a virtual interaction, which then makes them want to replicate that feeling in real life, in turn helping increase sales because salespeople are already anticipating the reward.

This type of gamification is about collecting data at key "challenge" points, tapping into the competitive nature of the player and not only making them feel good about their position (high score) but help them try harder to change their position (level up) and provide them with valuable rewards (SAPS).

> SAPS — Status • Access • Power • Stuff

It is interesting to note that stuff does not motivate people as much as status. When planning this type of incentive, it is important to think about what you want to give them as a reward to motivate them.

You'll see this type of gamification associated with things like loyalty plans. It is versatile among industries, and its greatest relevancy is when applied from a strategy perspective. Here are four areas where this type of gamification achieves real results.

MARKETING

▶ Loyalty programs — points for purchases
▶ Community building — points for engagement
▶ Conversion strategies — familiarity with product
▶ Campaigns with customization — greater interaction

START-UPS (Tech)

▶ Empty bar — getting people to "check in"
▶ Repeat visits — getting people to return to the site / app
▶ Vitality — getting people to share

HR / ENTERPRISE

▶ Recruiting — getting people to opt-in
▶ Onboarding — getting people to learn and integrate
▶ Training — motivate with a sense of progress
▶ Innovating — rewarding people for new ideas

SOCIAL CHANGE

▶ Education — getting people to learn faster
▶ Science — getting people involved in solving big problems
▶ Wellness — tracking movement and exercise
▶ Environment — getting people to game recycling

2) Collaborative Games

Luke Hohmann of Innovation Games loves serious games for the main reason that they are based on cognitive science and produce real results in the area of collaboration. The image below describes why games are great for collaboration and problem solving.

Goals

Constraints

Rules

Voluntary Participation

~ Luke Hohmann, Conteneo

Key problem-solving qualities of games include a shared and specific goal, constraints to maintain focus, rules to determine the right outcomes, and voluntary participation, meaning that people like to get involved.

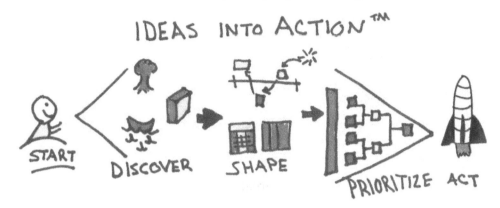

~ Luke Hohmann, Conteneo

Innovation Games is a set of 12 games designed to achieve very specific results and put ideas into action. There are three types of Innovation Games.

- Discovery games — help identify problems
- Shaping games — help get input on what is needed
- Prioritization games — help determine what is most important

Innovation Games have been called the "Secret Weapon" for lean startup by Hart Schafer because they allow you to obtain high-quality research at a relatively low cost.

When validating a business model, it's a common practice for startups to interview their customers. The benefit is that customer interviews are low cost. The drawback is the low quality of information. People answering telephone or solicitor surveys aren't necessarily pausing to thoroughly consider their answer and the effect it may have on data you're compiling.

You can build a fully functional Minimal Viable Product (MVP), but this is very expensive. The following chart shows how Innovation Games can give you great results for much lower costs.

Experiment	Confidence	Speed	Cost
Functional MVP	●	●	●
Concierge MVP	●	●	●
Functional prototypes	○	○	●
Landing pages	○	●	●
Surveys	●	●	●
Interviews	●	●	●
Innovation Games	●	●	●

~ Hart Shafer, Founder and CEO at TheraSpecs

These types of serious games are great for any type of meeting because they are set up in such a way that people feel able to have different kinds of conversations. Sometimes there are things that are hard to verbalize but can incorporate other tools like LEGO, improvisation, and storytelling to get to the real problem. They help drive innovation and collaboration.

> Other serious games resources to add to the Tool Box include:
>
> **Game Storming** — A Toolkit for innovators, rule breakers, and changemakers
> ~ http://gamestorming.com
>
> **Lego Serious Play**
> ~ https://www.lego.com/en-us/seriousplay
>
> **Tasty Cupcakes** — a compilation of business games
> ~ http://tastycupcakes.org

3) Experiential / Immersive Games

These games give players an opportunity to experience the results by playing the game as if it were happening in real life.

With an experiential-based business simulation, players make decisions, spend money, and see the results unfold. More companies are engaging in experiential games for conferences, where you play out a scenario and solve problems in real time.

Immersive games can involve more elaborate adventure. They might include costumes, story lines, and real consequences. Immersive games make for a very powerful business retreat, because you have to be willing to commit to the game!

There is a growing movement for Live Action Role Playing (LARP). This might represent the innately fun side of people more than the productive side, as its focus is on acting as another character rather than problem-solving. Yet, given the right set of people and an intriguing set of roles, even a LARP game has the potential to erupt into a world of new thinking.

> Two big players in the arena of experiential and immersive games are:
>
> **Frontier Trainings** — The World Leader in Experiential Business Trainings
> ~ *https://www.frontiertrainings.com*
>
> **Eagles Flight Training** — Organizational Behavioural Change
> ~ *https://www.eaglesflight.com*

From the Archives

I have both created and participated in several experiential business trainings that have offered profound lessons on human behavior, strong relationships, and an ability to test out new ideas and ways of doing things in a safe environment. It is better to massively risk and lose in a simulation than in real life!

The most amazing experiential business training was spending a week with 12 business leaders from around the world in southern France where we lived like Musketeers. This included riding horses for 3–5 hours every day and sword fighting for 1–3 hours each day with one of Hollywood's top sword masters. There were so many lessons on so many levels, including:

- *Communication*
- *Power*
- *Commitment*
- *Strategy*
- *Team*

I now incorporate these lessons into my consulting practice when I want to communicate without words, build strong teams, and fight for what I believe in.

~Muskateer Academy, Frontier Trainings, Gascony, France

PART FOUR

FOUR TYPES OF ADVISORY BOARDS

> "No matter how old we become, we can acquire knowledge and use it. We can gather wisdom and profit from it. We can grow and progress and improve, and, in the process, strengthen the lives of those within our circle of influence."
>
> ~ Gordon B Hinkley

OVERVIEW

Part 1 of this playbook highlighted the value and power of having an advisory board. Part 2 outlined the 5-P Process to build any type of advisory board. Part 3 was jam-packed with new tools and techniques to ensure your advisory board meeting maximizes results for everyone.

In this section we will consider in detail the unique requirements for each of the key types of advisory boards identified in this book.

There are four distinct types of boards: strategic, customer, community, and peer. These are the four majors, but each can be further customized for different companies at different stages of their growth. For instance, one type of specialized strategic board would be an innovation advisory board, built specifically for new technologies or products.

Given that the 5-P Process to building your board works as a universal model, this section will begin to identify the specifics for each type of board. We will examine and categorize each by the following set of criteria:

- Purpose
- Players
- Preparation
- Planning
- Performance

Purpose

What is the true function of the board? What are its goals, and how are they in line with the organization's ambitions? When this is clear, the working methodology has a solid foundation.

Players

Each of the advisory board forms requires the recruitment of different types of people for specific roles. Once you have identified the purpose, you can begin to compile your wish list of people who can best serve the purpose. For example, if your main purpose is funding, you will primarily look for the types of skills needed to raise capital, whereas if you need strategic advice, you will compile a list of subject matter experts for the areas where you need the most advice.

Preparation

Once you have the right people on board for the right roles, you have to prepare them for this very important meeting. You have to manage their expectations and make sure they know what is required of them. Clarity at this level ensures a smooth process. You must be sure they have all the right information so that their time is optimized.

The more the advisors understand the challenges you are facing, the more effective they can be in giving you the benefit of their ideas and suggested recommendations. This means feeling you have the right people and a solid process, so that you can open the books wide.

Planning

It is crucial that the meeting details — such as location, logistics, meals, and transportation — are secured, well-planned, and set in stone. You will communicate this information properly ahead of time, and by doing so you can take it off your mental plate and focus on the most important part: planning the meeting itself.

Part 2's Planning section reviews how to reverse engineer the meeting in collaboration with a professional facilitator to ensure a logical flow. This includes employing the right tools to achieve desired outcomes, accurately captured and translated into actionable results.

Performance

Based on the outcomes of the meeting, it becomes time to put ideas into action. This is what you've been waiting for! Team performance criteria will be used to measure the solutions to the challenges and their impact on the business.

Part of the continuous conversation with your advisory board is creating a communications and reporting program to keep your advisors in the loop and keep an eye on performance. Internal and external communications also benefit from strategies and product roadmap development. Especially if you are a startup, promoting your board of advisors can boost the value of the organization by association.

Strategic Advisory Board

Business Solutions

Purpose

Strategic Decision-Making And Growth

A strategic board of advisors is a group of successful business owners who have more experience and expertise than the CEO in specified areas and have committed to helping grow the business. It is important to understand that the role of these advisors is to help advise the CEO. The board is to hold the CEO, and management team, accountable. More importantly, they are going to bring a collective wealth of business acumen and experience that could help eliminate costly mistakes and also connect the business owner with contacts to whom he might never otherwise have access. These are people who have built successful companies and are experts in areas where you have business issues.

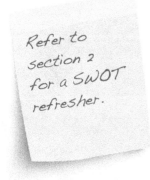

Refer to section 2 for a SWOT refresher.

First you need to determine the primary objectives for your advisory board, which will help determine topics to discuss based on the company's key challenges at this time in the life cycle. As mentioned, this could be funding, specific advice, or access to other industry leaders. To determine the purpose of your advisory board, begin with an assessment of the current state. I often recommend doing a SWOT analysis based on knowledge, strengths, and weaknesses, and determine your most glaring gaps in expertise.

The first step in figuring out who you want on your board is to determine where you need the most help. A SWOT analysis is a strong and effective method of looking at your needs, and you will end up with a very clear, current picture of your company. Because you are looking for strategic advice, you are looking for skills and knowledge that fill in the missing gaps.

Areas to consider when creating categories:

- Marketing
- Digital Marketing
- Advertising
- HR
- Strategic Alliances
- Franchising
- International Business
- Manufacturing
- Distribution
- Logistics
- Design
- Fulfillment

Players

If you are already experiencing success and your business is growing, you would be amazed at how many people are out there who would love to see you be even more successful. The kind of successful where you realize you know where you've been and where you're going.

Between you and your management team, you already know several business icons you could approach who have already helped build companies in a leadership capacity. Look for people who genuinely want to help, as their primary role is to help you grow your business by kicking it into high gear.

Board Members:

- 6–8 board members
- People looking for a 12–18 month commitment
- Willing to meet 2–4 times a year for 3 hours and up to 1 full day (at least one in-person and the others could be virtual)

Building Your Board

I recommend you begin by creating a mini "war room" where you have all your key categories you want to fit. Again, keep that list of categories to a maximum of eight.

The following are key steps towards building a strategic advisory board:

1. Brainstorm (and dream) a list of people who would fulfill the knowledge gaps / expertise you have identified. I recommend generating at least six names per category. Some may be wishful, meaning you know of them but they might not know you. If you get the feeling that having them onboard would be epic and helpful, that's good. Most should be more senior people, known by you or your senior management team, who have already given some advice as a mentor. You might also include a couple of up-and-coming business stars who have great ideas and are already experiencing success in their area of expertise.
2. Prioritize them in three sets of criteria that are relevant to the recruitment of the best candidates. For strategic boards, *experience*, *expertise*, and *connections* are all very important.
3. Once you have ranked the candidates in each category, it is time to reach out and invite.

One effective strategy is to go after the highest profile person who has already expressed interest in helping out and securing that person as your lynchpin. As you approach others, you can tell them this person is already onboard, and that may positively influence the next person's decision to participate. As more high profile people come on board make sure you use that in your invitation.

With strategic boards, it is usually most effective for the CEO to personally invite the prospective advisor either in person (including flying to a conference or meeting to convey the passion and commitment eye-to-eye) or with a phone call (sometimes through a third party introduction). These were outlined in more detail in Part 2 under the Players section. Follow-up can be done by letter or email. Note that there will be a significant time requirement from the top to get the right people committed to working together.

Preparation

Advisory Board Level

Once the members have accepted your invitation, you need to get them to sign a contract. Part 2's Players section provides a sample contract specific to a strategic advisory board. From that point onwards you begin the onboarding process. For a strategic advisory board, onboarding includes informing board members of the key touch points, topics, and your expectations with respect to participating and contributing.

Compensation

As a rule, when people are helping, there is not a big investment — between $500-$2,000 per meeting. For startups and smaller companies, a good meal and an interesting token gift may be enough of an incentive. If the company is growing and the advice is going to increase the growth and revenues, you may want to offer some sort of equity position and the trend is now more towards phantom stocks.

See Part 2's Players section for a reminder of phantom stocks.

There is a movement to make equity earned on contribution. Equity gets vested over time based on participation and contribution.

Information Package

Next you need them to really understand your business. It is important that the advisors help you focus on the future and how to grow, rather than spending too much time on where the company is now. Deliver a package of materials in advance that will give them pertinent information and highlight the issues on which you would like their help.

The package should include:

- Facts, specifics, and the real story
- Key milestones / goals achieved in the last quarter
- Key metrics and KPIs (or BGIs — Business Growth Indicators)

- Financial statements
- Key issues the business is facing
- Major decisions that need to be made in the near future
- Challenges and problems that need to be solved

Planning

Pre-Meeting

Often our tendency in life is to dazzle others with information about ourselves or our mission. If you do that in this case, you'll be spinning gold into straw. Maximize your time with the advisors by fully preparing them in advance. When they come into the room, you will reap the benefits of opening up your story prior to meeting. Get them to talk 80% of the time and only intervene to boost ideas, share further information to help the discussion and achieve real outcomes. You won't waste any of their time or yours by bringing them up to speed during the meeting.

See Part 3 for a facilitator refresher.

Facilitator

To allow you to be fully engaged in the meeting, it is imperative that you use a facilitator. This professional can help generate better conversations and keep the meeting on track while you participate. Facilitators are trained in character archetypes and how these personality traits can be matched to a type of board and its purpose. Look for a facilitator who has experience with strategic planning tools and techniques.

> Do NOT facilitate your own strategic meeting. You need to be fully invested and focused on the information you are receiving. Most business owners are not professional facilitators. The investment of a facilitator will help you harvest significantly more nuggets than you could ever do on your own.

Meeting Logistics

For this type of high-level group you want to make the environment as professional and high-end as possible. Consider a private club.

- Location should be off-site so that everyone can focus on the topics
- Boardroom environment with plenty of wall space for a potential projector
- Good quality snacks and beverages
- Celebratory and social event afterwards, such as a dinner and activity. Some off-site locations have great programs integrated into the meeting space.

Meeting Design

Always reverse-engineer your meeting based on the desired outcomes. Following is an example of how one might design such an outcome-based meeting. The proposed design will change if the outcomes change. Using the meeting design storyboard, map out one possible version.

The reviewed and revised meeting design will be the foundation for the official agenda that will be sent out in advance of the meeting.

MEETING DESIGN – STORYBOARD

STRATEGIC ADVISORY BOARD
(3+ hour - Afternoon meeting)

TOPIC	GOAL	GAME/ Exercise	WHY	STEPS/ Timing	LEADER/ FACILITATOR
Intro/Icebreaker	Set the tone and get to know each other.	Impromptu Networking	Get members focused on solving specific challenges and their contribution.	10 minutes	Facilitator
Review Current state	Set and clarify context	Business Model Canvas	Visual tool to review the company's value proposition and answer 9 key questions	10 minutes	Facilitator and owner
Review Current Strategic Plan	Articulate the vision and steps identified	BGI – Strategy on a Page	Highlight the major goals and strategies to reach those goals in all 5 key areas	10 minutes	Facilitator and owner
Problem Solving	Find the best solutions	Divergent & Convergent processes	Work to ensure that the group is solving the right problems first	60 minutes	Facilitator
Strategic Decision-making	Prioritize Next Steps	Analyses & Prioritization processes	Create a set of criteria that will drive the business forward and evaluate solutions by criteria.	45 minutes	Facilitator
Key Action Plan	What actions will drive the highest value	Dotmocracy or 20/20	Prioritize the next steps and rank them in what will help the company grow fastest.	30 minutes	Facilitator
Wrap Up	Continuous improvement	Retrospective Game	Set-up accountability for the Management team to the advisors.	15 minutes	Facilitator and owner

powerplay

Suggested Tools and Techniques

Strategic Thinking Tools

- One page solutions
    - Business model canvas combined with mapping the business model design space
    - BGI — strategy on a page
    - Gazelles — one page strategic plan
    - One page business plan
- Innovation and creative problem solving
- Liberating structures
- Shaping and prioritization games (innovation games)
- Dotmocracy (voting on highest value solutions)

See Part 3 for further outlining of tools and techniques.

Note: Time with advisors should be spent solely on finding and evaluating solutions for the business challenges set out prior to the meeting. The work that needs to be done to execute the solutions will be done following the meeting, with team members responsible for delivering those solutions. This is another key aspect a professional facilitator will be able to help you with.

Performance

Discovering new ideas, solving key problems and recognizing new opportunities are the value of having your high-level advisors around a table and creating an environment for collaborative and critical conversations. None of this matters, however, unless you put it into action. It is the speed of implementation that creates even more success.

Based on the ideas and strategies developed in the meeting, you will need to set a specific action plan and goals to make sure these happen.

As part of the wrap-up you will have done an exercise to evaluate what went well and what could be improved. These need to be integrated into the ongoing communications plan with the advisors.

The key teams that benefit from the advice of a strategic advisory board are:

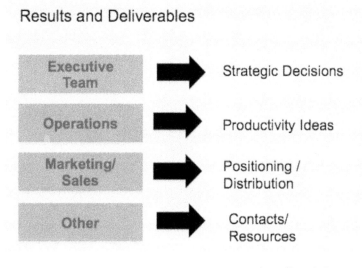

~ https://www.igniteag.com

Depending on the solutions, there are a variety of ways to use the results of the meeting to grow your company faster. The ideas can be incorporated into the existing strategic plan, and an external facing document can be distributed to key stakeholders to promote the key wins. The action plans from the meeting will be incorporated into the internal facing documents to ensure that the company achieves the key milestones you agreed upon.

Based on the milestones and key activities identified in the meeting, the progress of each initiative should be communicated consistently to the advisors. There will be follow-up meetings with the advisors, which will require an ongoing communications plan.

This is where accountability comes into play. As the representative of your company, you must demonstrate that it does all the things you said it would. You may have left your advisors with tasks, research, and new agenda items. Demonstrate you are holding up your end, and it will lead the way for them to hold up theirs.

Fortune is in the follow-up.

You've learned now that just 6% of small- and medium-sized companies have implemented and formalized an advisory board. This statistic refers to the strategic advisory type of board. This is how the other 94% of SMEs could have a significant impact on their overall profitability! There are almost 30 million SMEs in North America — an advisory board could be their secret weapon for accelerated growth.

Customer Advisory Board (CAB)

Marketing Research

Purpose

Marketing Research and Product Development

> *A customer advisory board (CAB) is a B2B business growth strategy. A CAB involves a regularly convening group of influential customer executives who have a vested interest in overcoming industry challenges and shaping the corporation's strategy. A well-designed CAB will provide a forum for peer networking while enabling all members to develop solutions to grow their businesses.*
>
> *A B2B CAB has many benefits, including increased understanding of the value a customer receives from a product or service, direct feedback on strategy and product development and the creation of strong relationships and enthusiastic advocates.*
>
> *Depending on how the board is structured, it can help increase customer satisfaction, co-create product improvements, and give insights into strategic direction.*
>
> ~ "Strategic Guide: How Customer Advisory Boards Drive Growth," https://customeradvisoryboard.org

All Tech companies talk about being customer-centric, yet very few of them actually talk to their customers in a way that gets them valuable feedback on their products. In the software development industry, it is very important to involve the customer in providing feedback on what is working and what they would find of the highest value.

Many software companies use surveys and customer "request" forums to help develop their product roadmap. This creates both confusion and the perception of differing priorities.

Neither surveys nor customer "request" forums really help prioritize the features customers truly value. Even a well-facilitated focus group of customers doesn't reach the real crux of the problems or offer a way for the customers to contribute in a meaningful way.

Large and fast-growing Tech companies, however, are successfully using a variation on focus groups. It is vitally important that these companies be customer-centric and offer innovative solutions. By embracing the CAB concept, using innovation games and other more interactive marketing research techniques, they are achieving great results.

By working closely with the company's biggest customers, a business can co-create and collaborate to continually deliver products that delight their customers. Many use a survey or have a dedicated page where the customers can give them ideas for improvement. As we saw in the area of design thinking, it is great to have a strong hypothesis about what a customer wants, but it is crucial to validate that with the customers themselves. Intimate and engaging dialogue structured in a scientific way will generate the best feedback and make very clear what the company should focus on next.

There is now a CAB Association (*www.CustomerAdvisoryBoards.org*), which was created "to promote CABs as a proven method for increasing sales, customer loyalty, and driving innovation in organizations worldwide." There are, however, very few companies providing training courses for CAB Management and Facilitation as well as best practices and policies. They tend to work only with very large organizations, which is why there is such a great competitive advantage for a mid-sized Tech company to get better customer feedback. While the "big guys" are investing $200,000–$500,000 per year on their research, by following the advisory board building process in this book, you can get similar results for a fraction of the price.

Companies with CABs have a clear understanding of what will drive value for their customers. Instead of building the product and then having a focus group to validate their idea, they avoid spending their resources on building something that is not important to the customer. In any business it is critical to find out what matters to your customers most and make it matter most to you. It's easy to see, therefore, why CABs are a growing area.

Players

When starting out with a CAB, many companies invite all their customers to a retreat and "wine and dine" them, give them lots of valuable content, and build their relationships. These are all good, yet do not provide real insights that will drive high-value product development.

> As mentioned in Part 2, there are different levels of maturity for advisory boards. In the beginning, many companies spend 80% of their time showing where the company plans to go, allowing only 20% of the time for input. This is often a question and answer forum. A smart company will set things up so that while they have those important customers together, they will listen 80% and talk only 20% of the time.

In a smaller, more intimate setting, you can find out more about your top customers than in a very large group. Instead of running focus groups to give feedback on product features and functionality that have already been built, think of your CAB meeting as an early stage think tank, where the participants can co-create and contribute to building a product that will continue to impact their lives.

Board Members:

- 8 board members
- People available for a 24–36 month commitment
- 1 face-to-face meeting every year (1–2 days) with ongoing communications and online meetings scheduled throughout the year.

Building Your Board

State an intention for your board, such as: a collection of key contributors who have a vested interest in making the product better fit their needs. Allow this intention to generate your general list:

- Customers
- Super Users
- Suppliers

This will be an ongoing relationship, not a one-off meeting, so you need a strategic recruitment process to ensure that you choose a well-balanced group of peers who will provide engaging and insightful information. From your general list, you can brainstorm who you already know, who you have heard about and are intrigued by professionally, and then narrow down your needs.

- Set the criteria:
    - ▶ What type of customer are you looking for?
    - ▶ What position, what size of company, what experience?
- Create a Target List
- Prioritize and Rank the potential candidates

Preparation

Once your advisors have accepted your invitation, you need to give them all the details of the meeting schedule for the next year and identify the time commitment for both in-person and virtual meetings.

Unlike the strategic advisory board, where you need to bring the members up to speed on the company first and on the specific challenges next, these board members will already be very aware of the product, what it does and how they are currently using it in their organizations. In the pharmaceutical industries, for example, CABs allow organizations to interact with physicians and their patients, who are the users of their products. The biggest requirement for your CAB is members who are experienced users of your product or service.

One often-cited concern is that the customers may all be competitors. This can be true, but the focus of the advisory board is to help everyone create a better product for that industry. Company specifics are not discussed, and the group facilitation is done from a holistic view of the product for the good of all.

Compensation

Because these customers are going to benefit directly from the improvements they co-create, there is generally no compensation. In fact, because some customers are so large, they participate and pay for all their expenses to attend, although once they are at the CAB event, all their hospitality will be covered. This is the industry standard, but you may want to offer travel and accommodations as part of the invitation package.

Planning

Pre-Meeting

Prior to the meeting you might introduce some of the techniques that will be used. You might request some advance feedback through a questionnaire or an online facilitated game. By highlighting best practices for this type of highly interactive meeting, you can set the tone and put the board members in the right frame of mind.

Facilitator

For a customer advisory board, you will need someone who is good at creating an environment. There is a growing number of good innovation games facilitators who understand how to run all the Conteneo Weave platforms, either in-person or online. One of the key responsibilities of someone using innovation games is training the observers to capture insights from conversations. These observers will be key people in the organization who are responsible for building the product roadmaps and developing some of the programming. It is very important that they listen and do not talk. As the customers become more involved in each exercise they will no longer be aware of the observers — kind of in the same way as reality TV participants begin not to notice the cameras.

Meeting Logistics

A key to success for these types of meetings is also to have someone on your team who is a professional event organizer. Not only will they ensure that all the required audio and visual aspects are looked after, but they will influence the theme and professionalism of the meeting. A well-designed meeting is an event.

Meeting Design

You will see from this sample meeting design storyboard that all the activities are different. Activities are focused on eliciting specific feedback for improvements rather than solving specific challenges.

For Tech companies, one of the most effective facilitation tools is Innovation Games. Conteneo, which is now the company that created Innovation Games, has created a combination of in-person and online platforms built on cognitive science that allows companies to mine lots of great information from their customers in a fun and engaging way.

MEETING DESIGN – STORYBOARD

CAB - CONSUMER ADVISORY BOARD

TOPIC	GOAL	GAME/ Exercise	WHY	STEPS/ Timing	LEADER/ FACILITATOR
Icebreaker	Get the participants interacting	Impromptu Networking	Creates a shared understanding of desired outcomes and gets people contributing	30 minutes	Facilitator
Discovery	Identify the #1 problem to fix	Speed Boat	Identify both the pros and cons of the product from the customer's perspective. Determine their biggest problem to fix	2 hours	Facilitators + Observers (trained in advance)
Shaping	Get customers to contribute new ideas and evaluate existing features	Prune the Product Tree	Get the customers to help map out what is important to them and also provide an opportunity to voice new ideas that are important to them	2 hours	Facilitators + Observers (trained in advance)
Prioritization	Get customers to Identify what matters most to them	Buy a Feature	Allow the customers to virtually buy the upcoming features – give them money but not enough to buy everything – what they purchase matters most.	2 hours	Facilitators + Observers (trained in advance)
Wrap up	Get feedback on the meeting	Retrospective exercise	What they felt worked well, what could be improved	30 minutes	Facilitator

p⏵werplay

Innovation Games

- A discovery game to identify any key problems to be fixed
- A shaping game that involves the customer in co-creating product development ideas
- A prioritization game to ensure that the company is working on the customer's most valuable products

Innovation Games®

... then consider these games

	Product Box	Buy a Feature	Me and My Shadow	Give Them a Hot Tub	Remember the Future	20/20 Vision	Speed Boat	Spider Web	Show and Tell	Start Your Day	The Apprentice	Prune the Product Tree
Customer Needs	■	■	■	■								
Requirements	■	■			■	■						
Product Usage							■	■	■	■		
Future Products		■			■						■	■

~ Hohmann, L., *Innovation Games: Creating Breakthrough Products Through Collaborative Play.*

Suggested Tools and Techniques:

- The book *Innovation Games: Creating Breakthrough Products Through Colloaborative Play* by Luke Hohmann
- The book *Gamestorming: A Playbook for Innovators, Rule Breakers and Changemakers* by David Gray is full of additional games facilitation techniques
- The book *The Surprising Power of Liberating Structures* by Henri Lipmanowicz and Keith McCandless

Performance

This information can be used by executives for strategic planning, by product management for developing the product roadmap, and by the marketing department to better position the product in the market.

Formalized follow-up and ongoing communications programs with your advisors are key. This is where your actions can create a chain reaction. Make it a good one!

Some ideas to consider as part of your follow-up plan include:

- online versions of innovation games;
- early and direct customer feedback; and
- techniques to further understand what is in the minds of your customers.

If the whole organization participates and contributes to the design of the CAB, then the whole company can benefit from the insights gathered during the face-to-face meetings and the other communications throughout the year. There are many benefits to opening up the design process of your customer advisory board.

The key teams that benefit from the advice of a customer advisory board are:

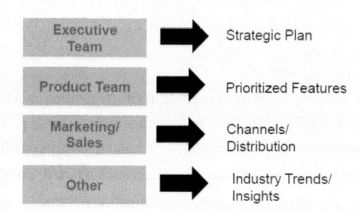

~ https://www.igniteag.com

Community Advisory Board

Volunteer and Fundraising Solutions

Purpose

Contribution and Camaraderie

A community advisory board unites people in efforts to bring about the goals of not-for-profit organizations, NGOs, charities, and any other group that is working for a cause. One might either have a hand in creating such a board, spearheading a community initiative, or be on such a board, exercising the opportunity to give back. They are often volunteer positions.

Volunteering to be part of an advisory board in your community is not just a way to offer service and make a difference, but it has also been promoted as a great offline marketing tactic. By taking a spot on a community board or committee, you will be able to network and work with other business leaders in your community. Based on the work you do for the organization, it is a great opportunity to showcase your skills and promote your business.

Generally, community advisory boards are for not-for-profits or charities. The purpose of the board is to identify high-value tasks that will drive results for the organization. As these organizations can involve a lot of talk and not much action, you must run a community board specifically and diligently to ensure results.

A community advisory board is typically a volunteer, working advisory board, which means advisors don't drop their advice off at the door and kick back until the next meeting. The organization should have committees, with advisors assigned to them. Being on such a board might involve fundraising, community events, advocacy, management of the projects of events, research and lobbying or implementing community-building activities.

In your own town or city, there are unlimited opportunities to give back. If you're interested in participating further with your community, an advisory board is a great way to engage.

One problem for a community advisory board can be a lack of sufficient engagement. Because of the voluntary nature of the role, people often fail to properly organize their team. Ensuring that roles are clearly defined, responsibilities are agreed upon, and meetings are properly run is essential to creating or being part of a community advisory board. It is essential to keeping the enthusiasm high.

Players

Look for people who live in the community and are willing to volunteer for your charity or community project. Any persons with areas of expertise are of high value, as they can lend these skills to the board and its specific projects.

Identifying potential community advisory board members comes from an opportunistic stand-point. Setting standards is an absolute. Keep in mind anyone with special connections who may be able to help further your cause, and don't be too shy to ask. You want passionate people who won't be afraid of a steady time commitment and won't back away from the action tasks associated with their role.

If you identify higher profile people, you'll need to be proactive rather than reactive in the recruitment step. People who can further your cause — who have a vested interest, can fundraise, advocate, and plan events — will be of great help to your organization's vitality.

Board Members
- 8–12 board members
- People available for a 12–24 month commitment
- 1 face-to-face meeting every month (or quarter), usually for 3 hours in the evening, with ongoing communications throughout the year

Building Your Board

State an intention for your board, such as: a collection of key contributors who have a passion for the cause. Allow this intention to generate your general list based on key skills:

- Fundraising
- Event and volunteer management
- Marketing and communications

Send as much information about the organization as possible when recruiting, centering on what it has done to date. Your recruitment package should include a one-page history with the key milestones, vision, mission, and values of your organization. Also include a selection of potential committees for board members to work on, demonstrating the task completion portion of the role and highlighting expectations. Once the member is on board, you can follow up with all the necessary tidbits of information about their committee, as well as the logistics of how the organization will run and expectations of their position. While the information you provide is for an advisory board member position, if the obligation is too demanding for people you've identified but they still want to be involved, they can join at the committee level.

Because these are usually unpaid positions, a volunteer advisory board mini-contract is suggested when onboarding. For instance, it might outline a commitment of three hours per month. It might include a performance criteria, such as not being absent for three or more consecutive meetings. It should include a status report to date of the committee they will be part of. The progress of the organization depends upon ongoing participation, so policies and procedures need to be clearly outlined and agreed upon at this stage.

Preparation

The logistics of advisory board meetings will differ for each organization, charity, or not-for-profit. You'll set the requirements according to your initial perceived needs, remembering that they can be adjusted in the future. The basics will involve the number of meetings required — monthly, quarterly, semi-annually — and the expected committee work, including reporting and accountability.

Community advisory boards are the exception to the "more than eight don't collaborate" group rule. These boards often contain between 12 and 15 people, acting as more of a working group than a think tank, with many tasks to accomplish. Meetings might occur in evenings in two- to three-hour blocks and involve light refreshments. Due to the volunteer nature of the position, not everyone will always show up. When schedules get hectic, the volunteer positions are often the first to suffer, which is why transparency around expectations is so valuable at the onboarding stage.

Compensation

This is almost always a volunteer position that includes a commitment to be a working member.

Planning

Pre-Meeting

Prior to each meeting you will need to keep the members up to speed on key milestones that have been completed by the staff and any other key deliverables from the members. This is also a time to reinforce the purpose and the progress, so that everyone has a shared sense of purpose and feels that things are progressing.

Purpose is the big driver here. You can never talk too much about purpose and vision, as they are the true home points of people involved in a community organization. When each project is put into the big-picture context, each member will resonate with the value of their contribution and perseverance.

Facilitator

It may be useful to have an outside facilitator come for an annual retreat-style meeting. The organization can look at the annual goals that will move them forward. At the monthly meetings, it is important to have someone who will facilitate the process of the meeting and keep it on track, but with a good system this process will be easy and seamless.

Meeting Logistics

These meetings are usually held in the boardroom of the organization or in a professional space donated by a member of the board. Most not-for-profits do have a board of directors as well as an advisory board and the board of directors may be quite heavily involved in these additional working meetings.

Snacks and refreshments should be provided for each meeting, as people are volunteering their time and expertise.

Meeting Design

When reverse engineering your community advisory board meeting, the outcome you want is straight-forward and two-fold: 1. Figure out the work to be done; 2. Figure out how that work will be done. You have a room full of capable volunteers whom you've worked hard to keep enthusiastic. Be precise and methodical in your approach, and your volunteers will benefit from your planning.

The meeting design in this case centers on giving everyone a voice. Each member is integral, as they have knowledge to bring home to the community. To stay on track and out of time-wasting mode, a stand-up style meeting is very effective. That is, each member is given a specified time to report the progress of their committee or endeavor and answers three questions with total transparency.

1. What did your committee get done?
2. What are they working on next?
3. What are the obstacles in your way?

The ongoing obligation of these questions ensures ownership over the advisors' positions and the necessary accomplishments of the roles. The rest of the board, the organization, and its committee members then all share the same level of awareness of progress and issues. From this transparency, members will walk away with top priority projects broken down into next- stage tasks.

MEETING DESIGN – STORYBOARD

COMMUNITY ADVISORY BOARD
(3 hour – evening meetings)

TOPIC	GOAL	GAME/ Exercise	WHY	STEPS/ Timing	LEADER/ FACILITATOR
Icebreaker	Get the participants interacting	Motivational Movers	Helps the Board understand what motivates each member of the team.	15 minutes	Facilitator
Purpose (review)	To ensure that the team is aligned with the goals of the organization	Purpose to Practice	Define the 5 key elements that are essential for a resilient and enduring initiative. (Working agreements)	30 minutes	Facilitator
Projects – development (PLANNING)	Make sure that there are clear expectations for the desired results	Work Breakdown Structure mapping	In a collaborative planning session, all the team members get a chance to understand the work that needs to be done and clarify the desired outcomes	1 hour	Facilitator and Event manager
Task and resource allocation (EXECUTING)	Get members to self-select and take ownership of tasks	Task Board & Stand-up reports	Creates a highly transparent view on what has been done and what still needs to be done. The task ownership creates built in accountability	1 hour	Facilitator + Committee Heads
Wrap up	Get feedback on the meeting	Retrospective exercise	What they felt worked well, what could be improved	15 minutes	Facilitator

p⦿werplay

As each new project in the organization begins, a longer meeting might be set. Include tools such as a work breakdown structure, separating the work components into smaller chunks — items to become part of the task board. Because tasks have been made into part of the volunteer contract in a manner such as "four hours of agreed work plus one meeting each month," each chunk of work could be divisible by four hours. This is how you assign work and these assignments are followed up on at the next meeting so that nothing falls through the cracks. With this type of design, people can have a tangible way of visually tracking the progress and the organization can celebrate each task, which creates a desire to do more.

Suggested Tools and Techniques

A combination of project management and team building tools and techniques:

▶ Driving Statement

This puts the project in context of big picture and the benefits of the cause. A driving statement provides purpose, which is important to help motivate the team.

▶ WBS — Work Breakdown Structure

This is a way to break down the work that needs to be done into chunks that can be delegated to the team. I recommend doing this as a group exercise to ensure that all the expectations of results can be accurately articulated.

▶ Project Task Board

This tool, which comes from the Agile project management methodology, is used to visualize the work being accomplished. Once the work has been identified, each member will choose tasks to complete and will move them across the board from "To Do" to "In Progress" to "Done."

▶ Retrospective exercises

These are ongoing exercises designed to continuously "tune" the team and make them more collaborative and productive. Every iteration of the project looks at what worked and what can be improved.

There are some low cost ways to turn these visual tasks boards into an online version that can manage the tasks virtually. One that most mimics the in-person Task Board design from an Agile perspective is Trello, an online resource (*https://trello.com*).

Performance

There are many personal and professional benefits of sitting on a community advisory board. It also helps the organization serve more people.

The key teams that benefit from the advice of a community advisory board are executives, management, volunteers, and fundraisers. The advice that results from these boards is illuminating for these groups.

~ Power Play Profit Solutions

Appreciation and celebration are major components of sharing in the mission-oriented community advisory board, so don't forget to incorporate hand-clapping and heart-felt thanks at every opportunity the meeting provides. And if that weren't enough, much of the work your board members do might be summarized in newsletters and campaigns that stem from committee projects.

This is the kind of recognition people like to write home about. It shows how their presence is having a true and significant effect on a positive movement. Depending on your organization, you may want to consider a volunteer recognition shindig, highlighting your advisory board. Does annual recognition feel right? How about monthly? Does a holiday card do the trick, or should you recognize your members on a project-by-project basis, giving other committees something to work toward? Whatever way you decide to do it, do it right — celebrate!

Peer Advisory Board

Formal Mastermind

Purpose

Solutions, Connections, and Accountability

A peer advisory board offers an opportunity to connect with like-minded professionals. Members help and support each other, access the power of collective thinking and group dynamics for better solutions. They are bound with accountability to the group and its members.

Setting to work on a goal or a challenge solo has one obvious drawback: it provides a limited amount of creative ability to solve the problem. You may be insightful, even bordering on genius, yet no matter how many directions you think in, you are still equipped with only one mind. The moment you onboard a peer, you have the effect of a third, more powerful element — the mastermind.

Masterminds were brought to the awareness of the public by Napoleon Hill in his book *Think and Grow Rich*. In this book, he revealed that many of the world's richest people in history were members of small (6–8) groups of peers who met on a regular basis (1–2 times per month) to share ideas, problems, contacts, and solutions. The term mastermind is relatively new, but the concept of people working out problems through sitting down with egos put aside has been happening throughout history.

> *The accumulation of great fortunes calls for power, and power is acquired through highly organized and intelligently directed, specialized knowledge, but that knowledge does not necessarily have to be in the possession of the person who accumulates the fortune.*
>
> *~ Napoleon Hill*

Peer-to-peer advisory boards function best with a pre-established theme. For example, they might be organized around a personality type and shared visions, a business area, a similar intended revenue goal, or a particular outcome (such as international expansion).

Some masterminds are a combination of customized content and specific problem-solving techniques. This type of peer advisory board has become more formalized with membership organizations such as Entrepreneur Organization (EO) and Vistage. They offer both content and peer advisory boards.

Benefits

- Networking
- Learning
- Accelerate business growth

Players

Look for people you know and respect and who are at a similar level of growth as you. Sometimes the people will gather based on their jobs, such as CEO, CMO, Solopreneur, or by their industries, such as digital marketing, sales, or fashion.

Board Members:

- 6–8 board members
- People available for a 6–12 month commitment
- Meet weekly, bi-weekly, or monthly (depending on the group) for 1–3 hours

More than with any other type of board, members must feel their commitment is sacred and show up to every meeting. Each member is a representative of their place as a peer. Missed meetings or a drop in enthusiasm will be felt heavily. I advise you to look for people who are there to give as much as to get.

Often, there is an application process, a contract and very detailed guidelines for the group. Based on the purpose and the values of the mastermind, the applicants are vetted by the organizer or by the group as a whole.

Compensation

Each member pays to participate, and this money will go towards the compensation of the professional facilitator, who will also be the organizer and content provider.

Preparation

A straight-forward tool to include in your meeting planning is a member binder. These matching binders symbolize an equal status from the start, and what you put in them provides an information and productivity tracking template everyone can refer to. In fact, while the binder will become what you give to your board members, it will also guide you through conceptualizing the board and its needs as you build it! Here are some items to consider:

- Meeting preparation forms:
  - Usually submitted to organizer prior to the event
- Action steps forms:
  - A way to formalize the work to be done between meetings
- Group Principles, Dedication, and Covenant:
  - This helps set the stage and hold the space for sharing and growth
- Member contacts
  - Stay in touch, grow relationships, and keep it positive

Planning

Pre-Meeting

The facilitator will distribute the details and homework prior to the meeting. There is often a communal archive of articles and other resources that is part of the peer sharing.

Facilitator

With a properly facilitated mastermind, the facilitator will act as the leader and will be responsible for planning and preparing every meeting in conjunction with the objectives set by the peer members.

There could, of course, be more temptation to skip on the facilitator for a peer group than any other type of advisory board. As a peer is an associate or co-equal, members might believe the equal balance of individual voices represents a peer board best. Yet as with any meeting, it is easy to veer off track. Someone with professional facilitation skills can bring the conversation back into focus and drive actionable results for all members of the group. Keep a facilitator involved and you will quickly prevent your intelligent, dynamic peer group discussions from dissolving into disputes and dinner-party conversations. It is also a lot of work to prepare and summarize each meeting and also look after all the logistics.

Meeting Logistics

These types of meetings are generally held in a company boardroom, a hotel business room, or in a restaurant or business club.

Meeting Design

There are several ways to run a peer group and because it is an equal investment arena for its members it has the potential to be pulled in one direction or another. Including some of the great qualities I have discussed — celebration, validation, contribution — can be tricky. As a leader, you want to make sure both you and your facilitator are conscious of recognition. Try the following design to maintain a successful peer advisory board.

Content

Depending on the theme of the group, there may be a specific program to move the business forward, or there may be guest speakers who come in for an hour. This offers changing dynamic opportunities to provide content that is applicable to the group.

MEETING DESIGN – STORYBOARD

PEER ADVISORY BOARD

(3+ hour – evening meetings)

TOPIC	GOAL	GAME/ Exercise	WHY	STEPS/ Timing	LEADER/ FACILITATOR
Success Celebration	Start the interaction with key wins	My greatest success this month was	It is important to acknowledge the goals that have been achieved.	15 minutes	Members
Content (Learning)	To give members new information that will transform their business	Subject Matter Expert presentation	Topic that will agreed upon by the group (depending on their business life cycle), presented by facilitator of SME	1 Hour	Facilitator or SME
HOT SEATS	Allow each participant to a chance to deal with a specific challenge	15-20 minutes in the Hot seat per member	In a collaborative planning session, all the team members get a chance to understand the work that needs to be done and clarify the desired outcomes	2 hours (6*20mins or 8*15mins)	Facilitator
Action Plan	Write down the key new actions to move business forward	Action Plan and Accountability form	When the new actions are written down and verbalized to the group – the probability of that happening is increased exponentially.	10 mins	Facilitator + members
Wrap up	Get feedback on the meeting	Retrospective exercise	What they felt worked well, what could be improved	5 minutes	Facilitator

p(>)werplay

Hot Seat

Our hot seat specifies who's on fire, figuratively speaking! This is a specific method of allowing each member to receive focused attention on their particular problem(s). If you tend as well as possible to these needs as they arise, your group will thrive.

The diagram below illustrates the breakdown of a 20-minute session. At the end, the member is in the hot seat with their own action plan in writing. They will be accountable for whatever they commit to for the next meeting. Some groups pick one member per meeting and give them more time to deep dive into their unique situation.

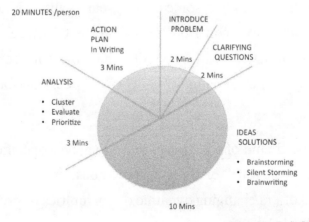

~ Power Play Profit Solutions

178   THE ADVISORY BOARD PLAYBOOK •

Suggested Tools and Techniques

- Mapping Tools
- Silent Storming
- Liberating Structures

Performance

By the time you and your board members have come to form a peer advisory group in life, you are already in recognition of unity through a shared unique quality. Imagine a group of artists who form a peer board with a commitment to staying involved until each artist receives public recognition or their first substantial payment for works created. They meet, share their passions, push one another, and provide information about who might best receive one another's work. They can speak out their frustrations and finally know their passion isn't disappearing into thin air through this powerful group of peer recognition. This type of advancement can only come about through the real magic of a mastermind — the fact that each member will commit to achieving a specific goal for the next meeting.

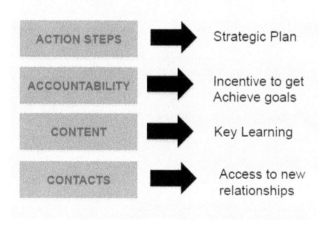

~ Power Play Profit Solutions

In business it is often hard to hold yourself accountable. That is why in a peer advisory board each member is connected with another member (for a pre-agreed upon time) as an accountability partner. The partners can decide how often they will connect and by what method. More and more literature has shown that you will get maximum benefits from creating a daily ritual of accountability.

> *Once I started working with my accountability partner on a daily basis, my success rate of achieving goals increased exponentially.*
> ~ Vern Harnish

ADVICE FROM THE ADVISORS

The Necessity of Collaboration

Picture a high school teacher administering a test and each student is expected to come up with the right solutions to the problem. In such a setting, some will succeed, some will fail, but few will solve all the problems. Those who do find the right answers won't share them with others. That would be cheating.

Suppose the teacher were to say, "I'm not testing you as individuals; I'm testing you as a class. Put your heads together and come up with the answers."

In all likelihood, no individual would possess all the knowledge needed to solve the problems or all the aptitude needed to apply the knowledge. But the class as a whole would have the knowledge and the aptitude.

Communication and cooperation would spread the knowledge throughout the group, and the problems would be solved. Instead of some people succeeding and some failing, everyone would succeed.

What is traditionally known as cheating in the classroom is known as collaborative problem solving in the workplace.

That collaboration is the key to success in today's global economy.

~ Dr. Nido Qubein

CONCLUSION

I hope by now the myriad benefits of having an advisory board — both for you and your board members — is something you're convinced of. You know how innovative and vastly different from a board of directors an advisory board is. You know the four types of board you can choose from to custom build for your needs.

Ultimately, it is a win-win-win business opportunity. Here's a quick recap of the wins:

- You win because the invaluable information and insights the board provides allow you to build better roadmaps that ensure greater results.
- Your advisors win because you offer them a safe and controlled opportunity to give back by helping your business become better, and they can possibly win financially too.
- Both you and your advisors win by expanding your circles of influence.

Your financial commitment can be relatively low compared to hiring or retaining high-end consultants and coaches, thus potentially achieving a very good ROI. However, it is important to remember that there is a big commitment in time on your part if you do everything on your own. By working with a professional facilitator and board builder you should be able to cut the time workload by 70%.

As we walked through the steps throughout the book, you've probably realized it's pretty straight forward and not hard to do. It can, however, be challenging to do it right, which is where an experienced and knowledgeable facilitator comes in.

Let's look into your future for a moment and assume you have determined the purpose for your board, so you know the outcomes and challenges you will address and solve. You have identified and recruited the best people to help you attain those outcomes. You have given them the right information prior to the meeting so that they have a clear understanding of the context. You have designed an engaging and results-oriented agenda and have brought in a great facilitator who will allow you to fully focus on the exchanges with the advisors and keep the meeting on track. You have captured all the great ideas coming out of the meeting and can implement many of them quickly. The more you can show your advisors you have done what they recommended, the more you will increase their belief and commitment to your business, and their vested interest in you and your company will be multiplied. Doesn't that sound exciting?

The advisor experience is going to be a big part of the success of your advisory board. The way you contact them, the way you prepare them, and most importantly their experience at your board meetings, will determine how fulfilled the advisors feel in their role. You want to be sure you are making the most of the time you have with them. That means you need to set up the agenda and interaction so that you can listen 80% of the time. Be sure you have told them about the key challenges. Finally, create the right environment for collaboration and innovation to flourish, and capture the brilliant ideas this collaboration will bring out.

By incorporating the latest interactive, communication, and facilitation trends into your meetings, you can begin to proactively engineer the results you want. This will make the most of everyone's time, not just in your advisory board meetings but also with all your other business meetings.

You've been introduced to many ideas from some of the top thought leaders in the agile and lean movements, such as:

- Visual Thinking using canvases, mapping, and other techniques to have better conversations and more transparency in communications;
- Design Thinking to help you prototype your business ideas;
- Divergent Thinking to generate ideas;

- Convergent Thinking to prioritize those ideas that create the best solution;
- Validation of these ideas with customers before you spend lots of money; and
- Gamification to add fun and serious play into your work and with your teams to increase engagement, productivity, and more creative solutions.

Bringing people and ideas together is key to our very survival as human beings. In a world that is moving at lightning speed, in which people are becoming more and more disconnected, it is essential that we reinvigorate our face-to-face communication and allow the wisdom of experience to be shared. This will help your growing business become more successful because there is a magical effect when people meet in person for a common purpose. It's your business, so create the environment for that magic to happen!

Ultimately it is not what you know but whom you know, and what they know, that matters. It is not just whom you know but the people with whom you have built strong relational capital, as that is the most valuable ROI for all businesses and business people. Those rewards must be for everyone involved. The secret ingredient to doing this right, to benefiting from this under-utilized business accelerator opportunity is having the right support in place.

Take action. If you reach out and ask for help and guidance, provide clear boundaries and structure, and create new relationships, you will get the biggest bang for your business buck. And it will be fun!

"A wise advisor's hindsight is your foresight."

~ Nancy Mayer

ABOUT THE ADVISORS

ABOUT THE ADVISORS

A note about my advisors for this book

THE ADVISORS

I thank all the experienced advisors who took time to speak with me and teach me about key elements of their insights on advisory boards. I am so grateful for your time and knowledge in helping me get this information out to business owners who are open to asking for help and committed to expanding their spheres of influence.

NOLAN BUSHNELL
Father of the Video Game Industry

Technology pioneer, entrepreneur, and scientist. Bushnell is best known as the founder of Atari Corporation and Chuck E. Cheese Pizza Time Theater. Over the past four decades, Bushnell has been a prolific entrepreneur, founding numerous companies, as well as consulting for corporations, including IBM, Cisco Systems, and US Digital Communications.

Currently, Mr. Bushnell is devoting his talents to fixing education with his new company, Brainrush. His beta software is teaching academic subjects in classrooms at over ten times the speed, with over 90% retention.

~ http://nolanbushnell.com

CHRISTINE COMAFORD
Passionate, Applied Neuroscience Guru

For over 30 years, New York Times bestselling author Christine Comaford has been helping leaders navigate growth and change. She is best known for helping her clients create predictable revenue, deeply engaged and passionate teams and highly profitable growth. As an entrepreneur she built and sold five companies with an average ROI of 700%. Comaford has been a board member for more than 36 startups and has invested in over two hundred companies.

Currently, Christine is at the helm of SmartTribes Institute that has developed the proprietary SmartTribes Methodology, which will transform you and your organization in three essential areas of Leadership, culture, and growth, and she is a columnist for Forbes.com.

~ https://smarttribesinstitute.com

BRIAN CROMBIE
Idea Sex and Ikigai Guy

Brian Crombie, Principal at Crombie Capital Partners, is an investor and executive with an MBA from the Harvard Business School. Brian has 20 years of corporate experience, a depth of knowledge in all facets of finance, strategic planning, and corporate / business development for a wide breadth of companies in several industries. Brian has deep political, community, and charitable involvement as well. A strategic corporate finance executive with M&A, VC, and PE involvement, Crombie has broad experience in Pharmaceuticals, Beverages, Entertainment, Hotels, and widely diversified conglomerates as well as not-for-profit and education.

Currently, Brian is the acting CFO for a sports team and part-time CFO for a development stage pharmaceutical company and an entertainment company where he also provides strategic, business development, and financial advisory services. Brian received the Queen's Diamond Jubilee Medal for his civic involvement. Brian has written and published several academic papers and other articles and videos.

~ https://briancrombie.com

JT FOXX
The Ultimate Millionaire Underdog

JT is a successful serial entrepreneur with companies, brands, and business interests spanning the globe. He is one of the top platform speakers in the world and has been deemed the World's #1 Wealth Coach as seen and heard on television, and in radio and print. JT is also a media and TV personality.

Currently, JT has started a Private Equity Fund Manager, an Investor in Properties & Companies, and is the Founder of MillionaireFlix.com the Netflix of business.

~ https://jtfoxx.com

ROBERT GOLD
The Technology and Finance Guide

Robert is known as a business advisor with great integrity, practical business insights, and passion for helping entrepreneurs, owners, and leaders achieve their goals. Since 2007, Robert has produced and co-hosted Canada's most successful business podcast — the PROFIT BusinessCast, which has a weekly following of thousands of business owners, managers, and leaders. Guests have included industry heads and thought leaders from across all industries, insight that Robert proudly shares with his clients.

Currently, Robert is staying at the forefront fintech and equity fundraising and still runs Bennett Gold Associates, which offers great services and resources for entrepreneurs.

~ http://www.bennettgold.ca

VERNE HARNISH
The Scale Up & Growth Guy

Verne Harnish is founder of the world-renowned Entrepreneurs' Organization (EO), with over 12,000 members worldwide. Vern is the Founder and CEO of Gazelles, a global executive education and coaching company with over 180 partners on six continents, Verne has spent the past three decades helping companies scale up.

He's the author of multiple bestsellers, including *Mastering the Rockefeller Habits*, *The Greatest Business Decisions of All Times*, and his latest book, *Scaling Up,* (Rockefeller Habits 2.0) has won seven major international book awards, including the prestigious 2015 International Book Award for Best General Business book.

Currently, Verne chairs Fortune Magazine's annual ScaleUp and Growth Summits and serves on several boards, including The Riordan Clinic, of which he is chair, and the newly launched Geoversity.

~ https://scalingup.com

HUGH HILTON
The Real Estate Restructuring Resource

Hugh Hilton is a founding partner of A&M CapRE. He is a member of the firm's board and sits on its investment committee. Hilton is an A&M veteran with a rare combination of corporate turnaround and restructuring, commercial real estate restructuring, and private equity real estate investment and asset management experiences. In total, Mr. Hilton has worked as a principal or in a key advisory role on over 50 real estate transactions with an aggregate value in excess of $4 billion. Mr. Hilton has been involved in 28 corporate restructuring, turnaround, and performance engagements at a wide variety of public and private middle-market companies.

Currently, Mr. Hilton is reimaging the creative office space, while A&M continues to deliver performance improvement, corporate restructuring, interim management, and business advisory services to companies and investors in a broad range of industry sectors, as well as to institutions and governments.

~ https://www.amcapitalre.com

LUKE HOHMANN
The Seriously Fun Founder

Luke Hohmann is the Founder and CEO of The Innovation Games® Company. The author of three books, Luke's playfully diverse background of life experiences has uniquely prepared him to design and produce serious games. Luke graduated magna cum laude with a B.S.E. in computer engineering and an M.S.E. in computer science and engineering from the University of Michigan. In addition to data structures and artificial intelligence, he studied cognitive psychology, and organizational behavior. Conteneo (aka Innovation Games) was acquired by the Scaled Agile Group.

Currently, instead of building a company to flip, he's building a company to change the world. His newest venture, FirstRoot, is a SaaS company and B-Corp. It sells schools a software platform and integrated curriculum that teaches financial literacy and civics.

~ https://firstroot.co

RONY ISRAEL
Business Development Yoda

Rony, is an accomplished international team-builder and strategic thinker. He looks for opportunities to assist small- and medium-sized enterprises to increase productivity and profitability. Rony has major accomplishments in management, including leading a number of major businesses for IBM in Canada, US, Italy, and for Unisys Canada, substantially growing revenue and profit. In Sales and Marketing, his experience includes developing and executing a very successful marketing campaign to position Astound as a significant player in the web conferencing and real-time collaboration space. In the area of International development and consulting, he has taken part in major trade missions to China and Italy.

Currently, Rony is the Senior Business Advisor, Advisory Services for the BDC (Business Development Bank of Canada), Rony has initiated a new in-house consulting practice that focuses on the provision of coaching and mentoring services to BDC clients and prospective clients. Operating mainly in manufacturing, knowledge-based, and services industries, these businesses are in the process of starting and / or growing their business. He has also developed a new methodology and program to assist clients form an advisory board.

~ https://www.bdc.ca/en

MITCH JOEL
Rock Star of Digital Marketing

When companies like Google, Starbucks, Shopify and GE want to know what's Now / What's next they call Mitch Joel. "One of North America's leading digital visionaries." Mitch Joel was President of Mirum — a global digital marketing agency operating in close to 20 countries with over 2000 employees (although he prefers the title media hacker). He has been called a marketing and communications visionary, interactive expert, and community leader. He is also a best-selling author, blogger, podcaster, and passionate speaker who connects with people worldwide by sharing his innovation insights on digital marketing and business transformation. He has been named one of the top 100 online marketers in the world, and was awarded the highly prestigious Canada's Top 40 Under 40.

Currently, Mitch is the founder of Six Pixels Group — an advisory, investing, and content producing company that is focused on brands, commerce, community, and what's next. Joel is frequently called upon to be a subject matter expert for *Fast Company, Marketing Magazine, Strategy, The Globe & Mail*, and many other media outlets. He is a regular columnist for the *Harvard Business Review, Inc. Magazine, The Huffington Post*, and other publications.

~ https://www.mitchjoel.com

JASON MORSINK
The CEO Turnaround Catalyst

Jason has a career rich in corporate leadership with global experience in North America, Europe, and Asia. Throughout his career he has been trusted by major corporations and global entrepreneurs to manage business development, growth, and turnaround situations. Jason has held senior and executive positions at global corporations such as IBM, TrizecHahn, and KPMG. For the past ten years he has worked on private equity acquisitions and restructuring projects.

Currently, Jason is an active angel and startup investor who seeks to add value to high-potential, high-growth companies with proven technologies and significant market opportunities. Jason is the CFO of several exciting projects, including PubLaunch that connects writers with the services they need to get published.

~ https://publaunch.com

DR. NIDO QUBEIN
The Articulate Educator

Dr. Nido Qubein's journey has been an amazing success story. The Biography Channel and CNBC aired his life story titled *A Life of Success and Significance*. As an educator, he is president of High Point University, an undergraduate and graduate institution with 4,300 students from forty countries. He has authored two dozen books and audio programs distributed worldwide.

As a business leader, he is chairman of the Great Harvest Bread Company with 220 stores in forty-three states. He serves on the boards of several national organizations including BB&T (a Fortune 500 company with $185 billion in assets), the La-Z-Boy Corporation (one of the largest and most recognized furniture brands worldwide), and Dots Stores (a chain of fashion boutiques with more than four hundred locations across the country).

Currently, Dr. Qubein is a renowned speaker and has received many distinctions including the Golden Gavel Medal, induction into the International Speaker Hall of Fame, and the Cavett, often considered the Oscar of professional speaking. He continues to transform and build High Point University.

~ https://www.highpoint.edu

GEORGE ROSS
The Legal Right-Hand Man

George Ross was executive vice president and senior counsel of the Trump Organization. He is perhaps best known as one of Donald Trump's two advisors on the NBC reality television program The Apprentice. Ross has more than 50 years of experience in real estate investment, and helped Donald Trump close his first deal at the age of 27. Ross and Trump worked together for more than three decades. He is the author of best-selling books, *Trump-Style Negotiation: Powerful Strategies and Tactics for Mastering Every Deal* and *Trump Strategies for Real Estate: Billionaire Lessons for the Small Investor*, which offers unbeatable insider advice for every serious real estate investor — beginners and old pros alike.

Currently, George is a highly sought-after business advisor and coach who loves to give back and is never too old to help groom new real estate entrepreneurs for success. He teaches courses in negotiation and real estate transactions at New York University.

ABOUT THE AUTHOR

Nancy Mayer is a profit strategist and business builder whose power-play approach has supported a multitude of client advancements, including leveling up to the coveted "Top 500 fastest growing company" status—a benchmark of real celebration. Her strength in building high-performing teams has recently been focused on supporting the advancement and proper-use of advisory boards. The joy and success for Nancy's approach to business is "Unconventional Experiences." Her proven outcome is increased *innovation*, *collaboration*, and *profits*.

She has developed thought leadership around 3 key factors for tripling revenues and doubling productivity; *Think* Differently, *Plan* Strategically, and *Do It* Faster.

She is a recognized international speaker, author of *The Advisory Board Playbook*, and is known for 3 cutting-edge foundations — *Visual Thinking* (canvases, mapping, and more), *Design Thinking* (prototyping and validating business ideas), and *Gamification* (using game design and thinking to make work engaging and fun).

Her own path of deep learning via unconventional experiences led her to a creative approach to advancing her clients in their successes. The following are career highlights who influenced her refined rebel style and vice versa: rock stars earning gold and platinum record sales, re-branding and building one of the largest music conferences in the world, helping the longest running motorcycle charity double their donations, designing and marketing award-winning sports and motorsports accessories, coaching software development teams for Canada's largest financial media company, lead strategy consultant for Canada's investment bank (BDC), coach for leading social entrepreneurs, entrepreneurship teacher at top Canadian business schools, and advanced motorcycle training to the US Marines. She has stayed as active and energetic in her work as the title Power Play suggests.

Nancy's unique toolbox combines traditional credentials with cutting-edge methodologies—Innovation Games, Management 3.0, Creative Problem Solving (CPS), Liberating Structures—resulting in a positive impact on the bottom line. Nancy is passionate about making the workplace more fun and bringing out the best in people. Happy, engaged people are more productive.

As active in her personal life as her business life, Nancy loves adventure and calculated risks like extreme skiing and motorcycles. She recently moved to the Salt Lake City area from Toronto and married her high school ski buddy.

The Power of Asking

It takes courage to ask people you respect to be on your board of advisors. I'm glad I asked my amazing advisors if I could interview them for the book (and get a picture).

If you don't ask, you don't get."

~ Stevie Wonder, American musician

ABOUT THE TEAM

The writing of this book has been assisted and directed by Stacey-Anne Curtis. Stacey-Anne is the founder of Pen Living. Specializing in writer and book development, creative expression, and teaching, Pen Living is a place to write the path.

Stacey-Anne juggles 26 letters each day. Her passion for the alphabet nourishes and facilitates higher skills of expression with those who are ready for a hand writing their great idea forward. She enjoys collaborative projects with purpose and is a poet.

The design and layout were done Downunder, thanks to modern technology and with Maria Biaggini collaborating to create Nancy's book. She is the founder of The Letter Tree, a small design firm that specializes in book projects.

When not working, she keeps herself busy painting, wheel throwing, and looking after an increased number of pets that she and her husband inherited since becoming empty nesters.